HOLY DARK PLACES

DANIEL MCGREGOR

Energion Publications
Gonzalez, FL
2017

TABLE OF CONTENTS

ISBN10: 1-63199-268-6
ISBN13: 978-1-63199-268-1

Library of Congress Control Number: 2017937638

Energion Publications
P. O. Box 841
Gonzalez, FL 32560

energion.com
pubs@energion.com

DEDICATION

Dedicated to John and April Heflick
Together we have walked in the wilderness
of each others' lives.

"The understanding is in darkness."
St. John of the Cross

Introduction: Liminality Defined and Prolegomena

C. S. Lewis wrote in his novel *Till We Have Faces,* "Holy places are dark places. It is life and strength, not knowledge and words, that we get in them. Holy wisdom is not clear and thin like water, but thick and dark like blood." What exactly is Lewis directing his reader to? How are holiness and darkness tied together as Lewis asserts? This book looks to understand what some might find an unnerving paradox of the Christian life and help the reader understand those "holy dark places" in both their proper biblical and historical context. In the discipline of Christian spirituality these "holy dark places" are referred to as liminal experiences.

Richard Rohr is the first scholar credited with designating the term *liminal*. For Rohr, liminal describes a time in which God's presence seems to be absent, the individual left wandering between destinations in the sea of life, attempting to regain his or her bearings. The term itself is from the Latin for "threshold" and describes the place between one side of a door and the other side. Rohr writes, "We have to allow ourselves to be drawn into sacred space, into liminality. All transformation takes place there ... where we are betwixt and between. There the old world is left behind, but we're not sure of the new one yet." (Rohr, *Everything Belongs,* p. 155). Liminal experiences exist in the in-betweenness of confusion and disorientation, and often precede stepping into a fuller and deeper awareness of God's love and presence in a believer's life. In an article describing Rohr's theology, liminality is defined as, "This bewildering phenomena, familiar in the Jewish and Christian Scriptures, [creating] for a time either contextual or inner dissonance which, when its work is complete, is often understood by the person involved as having facilitated considerable personal growth and change." In *Everything Belongs*, Rohr writes, "This pattern of falling apart precedes every transition to a new level of faith. If one is not prepared to live in that temporary chaos, to hold the necessary anxiety that chaos entails, one never moves to deeper levels of faith or prayer or relationship with God" (*Everything*, 158).

The first key toward providing a shape to the current project came in the form of an article by Anne Franks and John Meteyard, entitled "Liminality: The Transforming Grace of In-Between Places," published in the *Journal of Pastoral Care and Counseling*. The article is an overview of liminality and its basic definition. The article showcases the variety of ways to describe liminality, and highlights the need for further investigation. Within the pages of Franks and Meteyard's article is an overview of three biblical metaphors for liminality. These are rooted in either historical events (the Babylonian Captivity) or rhetorical devices (1 Peter's employment of the terms "aliens" and "strangers") that give tangible shape to the concept of liminality. The first of these metaphors is perhaps the most obvious, the wilderness experience. Whether the wilderness of Israel's journey to the Promised Land, or Christ's desert temptation, the wilderness is frequently used to describe spiritually dry periods. The wilderness captures the theme of leaving the comfortable for the uncomfortable. The second metaphor is the experience of the Israelites' exile and subsequent Babylonian captivity. The experience of exile would significantly shape and lay the foundation for Judaism for the next 2,500 years. The third metaphor Franks and Meteyard present is the "central spiritual metaphor" of the tomb or Holy Saturday (215-222). It is the notion that death itself is only an in-between stage for human existence. It is the "space between death and resurrection."

This book explores these periods of exile, wilderness, transition, and loss. The goal is to accomplish four tasks. First, the book aims to define liminal time and the existential experience of it by examples of it. Second, the book aims to establish a set of criteria for what counts as liminal events in a person's life. In other words, what happens in liminal experience that does not happen elsewhere in the life of the believer? Third, the project will attempt to broaden our awareness of both the biblical and historical voices who have spoken on the subject. This project is not a plumbing of one man's thought on the subject of liminality but rather a survey of helpful scholarly and devotional voices who have spoken on the subject of liminality in the past. The fourth goal is to lay a foundation for guiding and directing people through their own liminal experience. How might one best care for friends, family or parish members who are going through a liminal experience?

The first three chapters will examine each of Franks and Metayard's metaphors individually. Chapter one will mine the Hebrew and Greek words for wilderness as well as three key biblical examples: the Israelites experience after fleeing Egypt in the desert of Sinai, Christ's temptation in the wilderness, and Psalms 42 and 43. Chapter two will probe the biblical record concerning exile through the lens of Jeremiah 29, 1 Peter, and Psalm 137. Chapter three investigates our understanding of liminality through the lens of the tomb. This task presents unique challenges since the Bible does not contain anything like a full length exposition or description of the in-betweenness of life-death-life. Nevertheless, there are plenty of metaphoric and parallel examples of this experience. Two of these parallels examined in this chapter are found in Psalm 88 and Jonah 2. In addition to the biblical passages, theologians such as Hans Urs von Balthasar will provide additional context for a more in-depth theological plumbing of Holy Saturday.

The second half of the book consists of a historical study highlighting the variety and importance of liminality in the life of the Christian believer. This is in no way an exhaustive survey of Christian thinkers past and present who have ruminated on the nature of liminality and God's silence. But one of the goals of this work is to introduce voices and authors who speak of similar experiences but have had far too little attention paid to them as it regards the subject of liminality. As a result the book attempts to survey a range of figures and situations in which liminality maybe detected or found. The historical survey begins with St. Augustine's classic, *Confessions*, examining liminality at the moment of conversion.

The book then moves on to Julian Norwich and her *Revelation of Divine Love*. Third is another medieval mystic, St. John of the Cross, and his work *The Dark Night of the Soul*, a work which has become widely tied to the concept of liminality even if St. John would not have understood his work in such terms. Fourth, the book will examine the work of the pastor, teacher, and hymn writer John Newton, paying particular attention to his understanding of sanctification and the role of liminality through his "Omicron Letters." Finally, the book concludes with the 20th-century Roman Catholic scholar Henri Nouwen.

The last chapter will summarize what the book has explored and draw practical applications both for the believer and the pastor. The last chapter will help facilitate a greater appreciation and understanding to the experience of liminality including five significant issues. First, the location of the liminal experience is the human heart. Second, the broader context for this inner wrestling of the individual is the church. Third, the tools at the disposal of the individual in periods of liminality are prayer and pain. Fourth, the purpose of these times is to teach obedience, in order that a person may grow in Christ-like holiness. Fifth, obedience is then translated into action as the Christian obeys the will of God in his or her specific calling.

One final note of introduction. It would not be surprising if the term *liminal* strikes the reader as a strange or new word in the spiritual lexicon of Christianity. However, the concept of liminality does pervade our cultural context in surprising places. For example, writer, lecturer, and researcher Brené Brown writes in her book *Rising Strong*.

> ... [T]he middle space. It's not only a dark and vulnerable time, but also one that's often turbulent. People find all kinds of creative ways to resist the dark, including taking issue with each other.... Experience and success don't give you easy passage through the middle space of struggle. They only grant you a little grace, a grace that whispers, "This is part of the process. Stay the course." Experience doesn't create even a sin-

gle spark of light in the darkness of the middle space. It only instills in you a little bit of faith in your ability to navigate the dark (Loc. 627).

It is the intention of this work to provide the Christian pilgrim a solid starting point, both biblical and theological, in which to understand liminal periods, and their role in the Christian life.

BIBLICAL WITNESS

CHAPTER 1

WILDERNESS

Liminality is the space and time between departure and arrival. In the human experience we may look at this time as one to be celebrated and encouraged. Take the example of a high school graduate who is about to attend college. He is an adult in name but not yet in responsibility. He is dependent on family for much of his identity. This time can also be feared and hated. For example, the young woman whose husband suddenly dies is left between her old life of marriage and the new life that waits beyond her grief. The couple who grows increasingly isolated as they watch friends start their own families wonders when it will be their turn. In these cases they all know the destination, but they first have to walk through the vast space between to get there. The space is aptly named a wilderness, a desert one must cross to reach the safety of one's destination, where one belongs.

The notion of wilderness runs deep within the human consciousness. Being lost in a wilderness is often a main theme in works of literature, from science fiction epics such as *Dune* by Frank Herbert, to Homer's *Odyssey* (where the sea is the vast wilderness in which Odysseus is lost). Neither is it uncommon for themes of wilderness and desert to describe mankind's feelings of alienation from the world and from his fellow human beings. For example, T.S. Eliot wrote in his *Choruses from the Rock*:

> The desert is not remote in southern tropics,
> The desert is not only around the corner,
> The desert is squeezed in the tube-train next to you.
> The desert is in the heart of your brother.

It should be no surprise that there is a wide-ranging use of wilderness in Scripture. It conveys both a cultural and individual sense of loss and aimlessness. While paradoxically at the same time

Scripture also uses wilderness and the desert as settings for God's redemptive work. As the *Dictionary of Biblical Imagery* states, "This wilderness wandering becomes one of the central themes of Jewish history." The *Dictionary of Biblical Imagery* reflects, "Some biblical characters experience the wilderness as a place of refuge, while others are driven there against their will" ("wilderness"). As one might suspect, regardless of the reasons for being in the wilderness, it takes on a character and purpose that is unique to the biblical canon. Colin Brown highlights the wilderness's twofold nature: "The hope of eschatological salvation is also linked with speculation involving the [wilderness] ... at the same time the desert is a place of deadly danger, of separation from God, and of demonic powers" (*New Testament Theology*, vol.3, 1005). The route in and through the wilderness is always a necessary and often unavoidable one. As Franks and Meteyard state, "It is inevitable that one who accepts this invitation [to be in relationship with God] must leave the familiar and known to experience a time of transition characterized by uncertainty and unfamiliarity." It is just as certain that the wilderness is not the destination. Andrew Louth notes, "Perhaps the first thing to notice is that the [wilderness] is not an ultimate symbol: the [wilderness] is encountered in the course of the story many times, but the story neither begins there, nor does it end there" (*The Wilderness of God*, p. xx).

Franks and Metayard suggest that wilderness provides a natural metaphor for liminality. Experiences of chaos and confusion in a believer's life – often accompanied by a sense of God's abandonment – are nevertheless transformative. This chapter looks at several key biblical experiences of wilderness and attempts to tease out lessons and principles by which to enrich our understanding of this metaphor. First is the wilderness experience of the Israelites in the Sinai desert which lay the foundation for all subsequent biblical expressions of wilderness. Second is the New Testament's counterpart narrative of Christ's temptation in the wilderness. The third is found in Psalms 42-43, a highly personal and emotional response to wilderness. From these biblical examples of wilderness there are three important items for interpretation and application. First, these passages help draw out principles concerning the experience itself. Second, it enlightens the character of God who creates the wilderness. Third, lessons surface from the experience. However, before turning to the passages themselves, a brief examination of the biblical words for "wilderness" are in order.

WORD STUDY

The Hebrew word for wilderness is *midbar*, and it appears 244 times in the Old Testament. There are only three Old Testament examples (Deuteronomy 32:10; Psalm 68:7; Psalm 74:14) where a word other than *midbar* is translated into English as wilderness. *Midbar* can indicate a wide range of meanings: "… grassy pastures (Psalm 65:12; Joel 2:22), supporting sheep (cf. Exodus 3:1), sometimes burnt up by the summer droughts (Jeremiah 23:10; Joel 1:19-20), as well as denoting desolate wastes of rock and sand (Deuteronomy 32:10; Job 38:26)" (Kitchen, *New Bible Dictionary*, "*midbar*"). In general *midbar* is used for any expanse of land outside civilization and thus considered inhospitable to humanity.

The New Testament word for wilderness, *eremos*, only appears 33 times. The word occurs most frequently in the gospel narratives – a total of 19 times. The majority of these 19 are connected with Jesus and his practice of seeking the wilderness as a place of prayer. The emphasis in the Greek terminology is on the absence of an object in a particular location. The location is empty and abandoned. The absence can be that of a person, an objective and purpose, or cultural artifacts such as a city or human dwelling (Kittel, *Theological Dictionary of the New Testament, "eremos"*)

Colin Brown relates that the origins for the word *eremos* come from words meaning "to divide" and "separate." He further points out that in the non-biblical Greek the word may mean to "set free, to hand over, to leave alone." Significantly, the same Greek word *eremos* in the Septuagint appears frequently as the translator's first choice for *midbar*. *Eremos* appears in the Septuagint most often in Deuteronomy (in the wilderness experience of Israel); the personal emotional handbook of the Bible, Psalms; and, finally, in books connected with the exile of the Israelites in Babylon – Isaiah, Jeremiah, and Ezekiel (Colin Brown).

THE ISRAELITES IN THE DESERT

It is impossible to overestimate the importance of the Israelites' wilderness experience to biblical history. The wilderness wandering was the formative experience for the Israelites, repeatedly referenced throughout Scripture. From the time in the wilderness came the Law, a way of worship, and a culture distinct from their neighbors. In its sheer mass of material, the wilderness experience makes up nearly 70% of the Pentateuch, from Exodus 13 all the way through the book of Deuteronomy. Even so, the biblical depiction of Israel's experience is mixed. Frederick Tiffany notes, "The positive perspective is normally expressed as God's guidance of Israel, whereas the negative is seen in the rebellion (murmuring) of Israel against God" (pp. 55-69).

The wilderness wanderings follow on the heels of God's dramatic redemptive action in Egypt. "After the first great victory came the first big test" (Stuart, *Exodus*, p. 364). Douglas Stuart states, "Once across the Red Sea, the Israelites went to Shur. This is a vast, rugged, and sparsely populated wilderness region in the northern Sinai, stretching from what in modern times is the eastern side of the Suez Canal to the Negev of Israel." Stuart goes on to describe "a place full of dangers that contrasted sharply to their life in Egypt, where they thought they had enjoyed relative wellbeing." One of the Israelites' goals had been achieved – escape from Egyptian slavery and bondage; there remained the task of serving the God who made their freedom possible.

As dramatic as Israel's escape was, it was not long before they resented their living conditions and became troublesome. Stuart writes, "Remembering now what they had convinced themselves were the good old days, the people viewed the past differently from how they viewed it when it was happening" (p. 371). Indeed, Israel seethed with murmuring against God (Exodus 16:2) that was in reality an active rebellion against his authority (Ryken). Their request in Chapter 15 for something to drink was not sinful in itself.

Rather, their attitude with Moses, mistrusting God's leadership and his representative even as they knew very well what they asked of God in the beginning, betrayed the rebellious condition of their hearts (Stuart, p. 366). In contrast Moses took the proper attitude of faith as he obeyed God's commands without any personal reservations. (*Exodus*, pp. 366-367).

The wilderness became a harsh proving ground where God formed Israel's national and spiritual identity. Throughout the narrative one is able to discern God's working to accomplish several character building enterprises within the hearts of the Israelites. God was seeking to establish Israel's trust in him. As Ross Blackburn states, "The manner in which [God] provides for Israel further underlines the Lord's intention to foster trust in Israel" (p. 69). Indeed, according to Blackburn, "… the real issue is a fear that is born out of a lack of trust. God was pressing Israel to trust his leadership and to learn to obey his commands, thus this becomes the thrust of Exodus 16" (p. 70). Douglas Stuart summarizes God's intentions:

> God was testing his people throughout the exodus events: leading them in odd directions without fully explaining why (14:1–4), surprising them with potentially destructive enemy attacks even after they had left Egypt (14:10ff.; cf. 17:8ff.), requiring them to walk into and through deep ocean water (14:15ff.), and taking them to locations that lacked the necessities of life (as in 15:23ff. and 16:2ff.). All of these challenges were part of a plan to develop a people's willingness to trust him (*Exodus*, p. 374).

This process of instilling trust was aimed at developing Israel's willingness to obey God's every command; their loyalty to God was center stage. Regarding the incident of changing bitter water into sweet water in Exodus 15, Stuart comments,

> "What v. 26 called for was loyalty and obedience: loyalty in the sense of a willingness to pay close attention to what God's will was and to want above all else to please him by doing what he thinks is right.… God's expectation was sweeping. His

people must give him full, not partial, loyalty and obedience.
If he wanted it, they were to do it" (Stuart, 367).

And as Stuart further states, such obedience and loyalty came
with a reward – complete divine protection. Israel's obedience and
trust were necessary steps in order for larger and more important
things to take place in the life of Israel. As the Lord told Moses
in Chapter 19 of Exodus, "If you will indeed obey my voice and
keep my covenant, you shall be my treasured possession among all
peoples, for all the earth is mine; and you shall be to me a kingdom of priests and a holy nation." Such a calling required rigorous
discipline. As Blackburn observes, "The provision of the manna as
a daily provision is precisely meant to train, repeatedly instilling
in Israel the kind of trust in the Lord that is so foundational in
preparation for the giving of the law" (Blackburn, 69).

Through the wilderness, God was also instilling a sense that
ultimately it was he who was leading Israel in every moment of
their journey. "God was teaching them a concept: that he was
their ultimate provider, the one who from heaven gave them not
necessarily what they expected but what they really needed" (Stuart,
372). As Fredrick Tiffany points out, "God provides a way through
the desert. The chaos of the wilderness poses no real threat; neither
does it need to be the occasion of struggle. The Lord is in control,
and a people has been formed. With the defeat of chaos comes the
creation of a new people" (Tiffany).

If Israel did not learn its lesson perfectly, it did come away
changed and significantly shaped by the experience. Colin Brown
writes, "Israel's forty years of wandering in the wilderness was
counted as a time of particular closeness to Yahweh" (O. Bocher,
New International Dictionary of New Testament Theology, p. 1005).
Andrew Louth states, "The period of the wandering in the wilderness, in contrast to the period that followed when, according to the
biblical account, the Israelites began to settle in Palestine, is often
regarded by the later prophetic tradition as a golden age" (*Wilderness*, p. 33). The wilderness experience became part of the ritual
life of the community. Once a year all of Israel would live in a tent
in the wilderness during the feast of Tabernacles. The narrative of

Israel's history would be profoundly altered if it were not for their time in the desert.

One can easily imagine the parallels in the lives of ordinary believers. Often enough individuals – after the fact – count periods of lost-ness and struggle as often being particularly sweet times of God's presence – individual lives playing out the experience of the Israelites in miniature.

Jesus's Temptation

The temptation of Jesus appears in all three synoptic gospels, albeit in dramatically varying lengths. Matthew's account is in Chapter 4 verses 1-11. Mark barely mentions the temptation, giving it a scant two verses (verse 12-13) in the first chapter of his narrative. Finally, Luke devotes the first 13 verses of Chapter 4 to the encounter. In all three accounts it is set as a contrast to the failures of Israel. Christ's temptation experience thus offers a picture of covenant faithfulness. Where others have failed, Jesus succeeds.

> "The most significant key to the understanding of this story is to be found in Jesus's three scriptural quotations. All come from Deut. 6-8, the part of Moses's address to the Israelites before their entry into Canaan in which he reminds them of their forty years of wilderness experiences.... There in the wilderness he, too, faces those same tests, and he has learned the lesson which Israel had so imperfectly grasped" (France, *Matthew*, 127).

Another commentator argues the temptation of Jesus contains interesting parallels with the story of Adam and Eve in the opening saga of Genesis. "Interesting parallels emerge between Jesus' three temptations and those of Eve and Adam in the garden (Genesis 3:6 – 'good for food,' 'pleasing to the eye,' 'desirable for gaining wisdom'). Both of these triads seem to parallel John's epitome of human temptation: 'the lust of the flesh and the lust of the eyes and the pride of life' (1 John 2:16, RSV)" (Blomberg, *Matthew*, p. 87).

Like the Children of Israel, Jesus's temptation in the wilderness is preceded by a public display of God's power and confirmation

of the calling into ministry. R. T. France writes, "The special relationship with God which has just been authoritatively declared at
the Jordan is now under scrutiny" (France, *Matthew*, p. 127). Just
as with the children of Israel, the desert experience was essential
for Jesus and his ministry. "It was a great source of his humanness
as well as his holiness. Even after he left the wilderness, he carried
it around inside of him, and far from fleeing it later in his life he
sought it out. Without the wilderness he might not have been the
same person. Because of the wilderness he was not afraid of anything" (Taylor, "Four Stops in the Wilderness," pp. 3-9). Jesus's
temptations come, as Matthew recounts, at his weakest, when he
has already spent 40 days alone and without food (Matthew 4:2).
The account in Luke suggests that the temptations had already been
in progress for 40 days when at the end of this period Satan tempted him with three specific barbs (Luke 4:2). In either case, "The
most likely emphasis [in the temptation narrative] is on deliberate
self-deprivation to facilitate exposure to one's self of the nature
of the self before God: the pressure of hunger can be immensely
self-revealing. In this way fasting plays a role in bringing the issues
facing Jesus into sharp focus" (Nolland, *The Gospel of Matthew*, p.
162). Luke's language suggests that it was Jesus's obedience to God
the Father that was in question. As I. Howard Marshall states, the
Greek verb, in the Lucan context, "means 'to test someone,' and it is
used in the OT... of God testing men in order to assess the reality
of their faith and obedience" (Marshall, *Luke*, p. 169).

Mark's account of the temptation may be a sliver of the length
of its counterparts. However, it contributes at least one significant
insight on the nature of Christ's wilderness experience. The verb
Mark puts in his text is crucial to understanding that this encounter
is in fact a Spirit-led and -driven occurrence. Mark uses the more
vivid verb *ekballw* (to throw out) declined in the historic present
tense to add to the immediacy of the word's impact. While it would
be an exaggeration to say that *ekballw* always suggests violence (it
does not in Matthew 9:38; John 10:4; James 2:25), it normally
implies at least the possibility of resistance. The majority of uses
in Mark are of expelling demons from individuals. This turn of

events is unexpected here, where Jesus's willing acceptance of his God-given mission has been clearly implied in the text; even so, it perhaps serves to underline the seriousness of the coming conflict which will be inaugurated between Christ and the devil (France, *Mark*, 84-85).

The temptation narrative contains three tests of Christ's faithfulness to his Father. According to the Matthew account the first test relates to his physically weakened state. The second focuses on his calling and identity. The third concerns who Christ would worship – the power Satan offered, or his heavenly Father. Craig Blomberg explains by writing, "The devil tries to seduce him with instant power, authority, and wealth apart from the way of the cross.... But the devil's price is damning. He requires nothing short of selling one's soul in worshiping him, which leads inexorably to eternal judgment" (Blomberg, 85). These three temptations, recorded in Matthew and Luke, are meant to dig at the core of what it is to be human. Nouwen believes that Jesus's three temptations represent the three great potential vulnerabilities of those who would truly follow God: the need to be relevant; the need to be significant; the need to be powerful" ("Liminality," pp. 215-222). Even as such, Jesus understands heavenly truths trump Satan's lies.

It is important to note that what had been the scene of struggle and conflict in the aftermath becomes for Jesus a place of refuge and serenity. Over the course of his ministry, Jesus would time and time again enter the wilderness or desert to pray and commune with his Father. For example, Luke 5:15-16 says, "But now even more the report about him went abroad, and great crowds gathered to hear him and to be healed of their infirmities. But he would withdraw to desolate places and pray." And Mark 6:46 states, "And after he had taken leave of them, he went up on the mountain to pray." Once the struggles of the desert are faced and conquered, it becomes a place of strength and refuge.

PSALM 42-43

The opening two psalms of the second book of the psalms, 42 and 43, are considered by most scholars to be one psalm comprised of three strophes (42:1-5, 6-11, and 43:1-5). There are three reasons for this conclusion. First, Psalms 42 and 43 are joined together in the Hebrew manuscripts. Second, every psalm in the second collection, with the exception of Psalms 71 and 43, has an introductory title. And finally, the same refrain is repeated three times between the two psalms (42:5, 11; 43:5). It is also the first of the elohistic psalms, which use the more general term "Elohim" for God (Waltner, p. 219). One commentator noted these psalms "reflect the dark night of the soul" for the psalmist and as a result remain two of the more popular psalms in the cannon (Waltner, p. 219). Geoffrey Grogan states, "There is great emotional depth too in this lament, somewhat as in the book of Job, where complaints to God alternate with assertions of confidence in him" (Grogan, p. 96). As dark as the veil is over the psalmist, he continues in a positive refrain of trust, and the phrase "hope in God" appears three times at the end of each strophe (42:5, 42:11 and 43:5) (Bratcher, p. 398).

The author of Psalms 42 and 43 is a temple musician who was responsible for leading Israel in worship. His lament is a looking back at the past experiences of success while at the same time wrestling with his current circumstances and finally looking forward to God's redemptive power. The first strophe can be summarized as a meditation on the past: "these things I remember" (42:4). Its image of drought heightens the sense of homesickness and loss which the psalmist is feeling. The second strophe is focused on the present troubles and feelings of despair; the psalmist is confronted not only with his own inner angst, but also with the taunts of his enemies. Psalm 43, which is the entire last strophe, focuses on the future as it calls out to God, "Vindicate me, O God...." The thrust is the psalmist's plea for deliverance from woe.

There is disagreement amongst scholars whether the physical location referred to in Psalms 42 and 43 is to be taken literally or merely as poetic devise to strengthen the sense of alienation and disconnect. However, if one does take the location to be an actual place it is important to note, "He is at the furthest remove in Israel from Jerusalem, at Jordan's headwaters on mighty Mount Hermon. Its tumultuous, dangerous cataracts, linked in his imagination with even greater dangers at sea, are frightening, yet the repeated 'your' (v. 7) perhaps shows hope, for even nature's most threatening manifestations are under God's control" (Grogan, 97). Grogan continues by observing that "His [the psalmist's] geographical remoteness from God's house (vv. 2, 4) is agonizing, comparable to an animal's desperate thirst for water" (Grogan, p. 96).

As with all psalms, the author of 42 and 43 presents a wide range of strong feelings on the subject at hand. The phrase "I pour out my soul" in verse four could be more accurately translated as "give expression to my pent-up feelings" (Anderson, p. 331). Eugene Peterson's *The Message* paraphrases the verse as, "These are the things I go over and over, emptying out the pockets of my life" (Peterson, Psalm 42:4). Three clear negative emotions are expressed in the lines of these two psalms: longing, confusion, and depression.

James Limburg diagnoses the author's problem as one of needing to return to what is comfortable for him. "The psalmist's problem could be diagnosed as homesickness, a deep longing to be back in familiar places with the family of God and, in fact, to be back with God" (Limburg, p. 142). Accompanying these desires is the feeling that God has abandoned him to his fate. The psalmist is "feeling forgotten by God and being harassed by the people around him" (Limburg, p. 142). The longing and abandonment generate in the psalmist both the feeling of needing God to silence his opponents, as well as the need for God to renew his presence with the psalmist.

Into these feelings of homesickness and abandonment comes the psalmist's confusion and anger concerning his present circumstances. "There is a roaring going on inside him, like the roaring of the waves of the sea (Jeremiah 5:22), that will not be calmed" (Limburg, p. 143). This is especially on display in the second strophe as the author asks, "Why are you downcast, O my soul, and why are you in turmoil within me?" (Psalm 42:5). This period of forced absence from the temple is causing him to call everything into question. As James Montgomery Boice states, "So the author's forced absence from Jerusalem was also an absence from his work and therefore from his sense of being useful. It reflected on his whole purpose for living" (Boice, p. 368).

Finally, the longing for home, added with his feelings of confusion and anger, leads to a spiritual depression. Once again Boice provides the reader with the necessary interpretation of the psalmist's plight, suggesting six causes within these psalms which have encouraged this state of affairs (Boice, pp. 367-369). First, as mentioned above, is the forced absence from the temple (42:1-2). Second are the taunts of unbelievers (42:3, 10). Third, the memories of the "good old days" worshipping at the temple become burdensome to the psalmist (42:4). Fourth is the overwhelming trial of his current condition (42:7). Fifth is God's absence or failure to act quickly on behalf of his servant (42:9). And finally, not only is the psalmist faced with those who mock him, but he is faced with the attacks from deceitful and wicked persons (43:1).

What then is the remedy? How does the psalmist continue to go on? Two things sustain him as he journeys through this time in his life. One is a positive use of memory: he recounts God's faithfulness to him. Second, he focuses exclusively on God and worship of God in the midst of his condition. The "I remember" of verse four is not entirely a stinging rebuke. "This is not an accidental recollection but a deliberate attempt to call to mind certain past events.... Although separated from the Temple and all the ritual, he can participate in the salvation-history through memory of the mighty works of God" (Anderson, p. 330). As another commentator states, "We also notice that the one in such desperate straits looks to the past, remembering the good times.... Remembering what God has done in the past somehow seems to help with the difficulties of the present" (Limburg, p. 144. See also Psalm 22). Even as the memories may sting, the process of remembering becomes his antidote to depression: "'Therefore I remember thee:' this is the psalmist's antidote to despair and depression, even though it may increase the sharpness of his agony" (Anderson, p. 329).

Finally, for the psalmist, the answer to his trouble lies in the person of God; the psalmist repeats three times the refrain, "hope in God." Just as the Israelites were meant to find their hope and salvation in God during the wilderness wanderings and just as Jesus successfully remained focus on the true object of worship, the psalmist finds that his answer is in God alone. "So in his despondency he finds joy in God himself. The reiterated use of God's name and of the possessive pronoun gives emotional depth to this verse" (Grogan, p. 97). The psalmist finds – as Christ did centuries later – that spiritual truth trumps despair and disobedience.

CONCLUSION

Franks and Metayard state that the wilderness, as a metaphor for liminal experience, has at least two clear parallels. First, the Israelites journey from slavery and relative comfort in Egypt to discomfort and freedom in the desert ("Liminality," pp. 215-222). Franks and Metayard's second point is that in the desert "the people of Israel were given opportunity to experience the power and presence of God first-hand" ("Liminality"). Indeed, whatever else can be said about liminal experience and its connection with the wilderness, it is certain to disrupt the life of an individual, causing him or her to be exposed to God's transformative presence. Barbara Taylor summarizes the condition in which people find themselves in the wilderness:

Whatever your own wilderness is like, I am betting that it has at least three things in common with all other wildernesses: You did not choose it. It is no place you would ever have gone on your own. You are not in control. You cannot even control the pounding of your own heart (Taylor, pp. 3-9).

First and foremost, wilderness experiences – and by inference liminal experiences – exist to draw the individual to abandon control of his or her life. Andrew Louth observes, "The desert symbolizes the relinquishing of human concerns so that God alone can be their sole concern.... That is the first lesson the desert teaches; relinquishment of human society and human control and dependence on God alone" (*Wilderness*, p. 29). C. H. Spurgeon notes that "He whose life is one even and smooth path, will see but little of the glory of the Lord, for he has few occasions of self-emptying" (Spurgeon, *Morning and Evening*, p. 402). One wonders whether this is a commentary on the hard-heartedness of mankind that such drastic action is needed, or on the lengths to which God is willing to go in order to reclaim mankind's hearts.

Second, the physical reality of the wilderness is trumped by the spiritual reality involved. As seen in the narrative of Jesus's temptation in the wilderness, it is the scriptural and spiritual truth that is able to overcome Satan's powerful physical temptations. Liminal experiences are by default difficult periods to transverse. However, as difficult as these periods are, pastors need to remind their congregations that the spiritual reality is greater than the natural. The Jesus narrative also alludes to the importance of Scripture in the midst of the wilderness experience. It is primarily Scripture, not only his own will to resist, that Christ wields to combat the temptations he faces in the wilderness. This ought to give the reader pause to consider the importance not only of worship (rich in the reading of Scripture), but also the memorization of Scripture.

Third, the wilderness experience, like any liminal experience, is merely a moment in time that will pass away. The wilderness is not a permanent destination but rather a crucible that forms the individual for the task ahead. For Israel in Exodus it is the creation and formation of a nation. Christ in the desert was prepared for the ministry that would eventually lead to the cross and the ransom of mankind. And for the psalmist, the experience ends in a return to the worship of God at the temple. Thus it might be suggested that an experience is not truly liminal without there being some greater purpose on the other side of it.

Through the midst of the wilderness experience, the aim is for the individual to trust God and to obey him completely. No matter how strange or difficult the task or request, God is looking in the desert to see people faithfully respond to him. Thus, as in the psalmist's prayer, the desert experience fosters right worship and a greater intimacy with the God who brought the individual there in the first place. One must at this point recognize that the wilderness – despite what one would like – is a necessary part, and indeed a desperately needed part, of the Christian journey.

Chapter 2

Exile

For many individuals, exile is a frightening prospect one hopes never to have to suffer. It conjures the forced removal of what is safe, comforting, and familiar. In many ancient cultures, such as Rome and the Babylonians, exile was a devastating political punishment. Franks and Meteyard state that the metaphor of exile communicates "the experience of being forced to leave home country and take up residence in a foreign land" ("Liminality"). As the *Dictionary of Biblical Imagery* states, "Exile encompasses a social role involving fringe status and a psychological state that includes as its salient features a sense of loss or deprivation and a longing to return to (or arrive at) a homeland.... Above all, the exile is a displaced person" (Ryken, *Dictionary of Biblical Imagery*, "exile").

Apart from being a metaphor of liminality, exile is an important theme within the biblical canon. This is true in two senses. First, exile is an important historical event. The exile of 597 B.C. is one of the two great defining events in the life of the Jewish people, the second and earlier event being the Exodus. Andrew Mein states the exile to Babylon "set a pattern whereby those living away from the land of Israel could maintain a distinct religious and cultural identity" (Mein, *Ezekiel and the Ethics of Exile*, p. 40). The second sense in which exile is important in its biblical context is the way it is used as a literary motif. Within the canon of Scripture there are numerous examples of exile. It was a favorite image for writers in both Testaments. As Walter Brueggemann describes, "It is clear that 'exile' is a rich and supple metaphor. As the biblical writers turned the metaphor of exile in various and imaginative directions, so may we." (Brueggemann, *Cadences of Home*, p. 11). In both the Old and New Testament, numerous individuals found themselves exiles or exiled. The most notable examples outside of the Babylonian captivity include: Adam and Eve's exile from the garden, Cain's exile, Joseph's exile to Egypt, Moses' exile from Egypt, Christ's exile in Egypt, and the Apostle John's exile to the island of Patmos. Not all of the exiles in the Scriptures had negative experiences. In the case of Ruth her exile from her homeland resulted in her marriage to Boaz.

It is therefore necessary to limit our investigation of exile and focus on a small number of representative texts. The first step is to examine the original Hebrew and Greek words for "exile." The objective is to discover what, if anything, the etymology of the word tells us about the use of exile as a metaphor concerning our spiritual journey. Second, we will look at three passages of Scripture that each approach exile from a different point of view. Jeremiah 29 records Jeremiah's advice to the exiles in Babylon – challenging them to not be idle in their experience in a foreign land. First Peter and the example of John the Divine represent the New Testament contribution to our understanding of exile. The last passage will be Psalm 137, a song of exile, expressing the emotional response of those in exile. Exile in these passages of Scripture provides substantial clues as to how an individual should conduct him or herself in the experience of liminality.

HEBREW AND GREEK WORD STUDY

The word "exile" appears 97 times in the *English Standard Version,* and 102 times in the *New Revised Standard Version* in the Old and New Testaments. In the Old Testament the most common word translated as exile is *golah.* The verbal root word for *golah* in its original context means to "uncover," to "expose," or "to reveal." There are only three exceptions where "exile" is found in the Old Testament and the Hebrew word *golah* is not used. In Nehemiah 1:2 and 1:3 the emphasis is on the state of captivity and confinement and therefore the Hebrew word is different. The third exception is in Isaiah 27:8 where the emphasis is on the act of sending one forth into exile. In total, the word *golah* is found 187 times in the Old Testament. *Golah* is translated 97 times directly as "exile" in the text. For example, in Job 12:22 the root is translated as "He *uncovers* the deeps out of darkness and brings deep darkness to light" Isaiah uses the same word in 5:13, "Therefore my people *go into exile* for lack of knowledge; their honored men go hungry, and their multitude is parched with thirst." *Golah* is used four times in Jeremiah 29, each time translated as exile. However, there is one instance, in Jeremiah 49:10, where the same word is translated as "exposed": "But I have stripped Esau bare; I have *uncovered* his hiding places, and he is not able to conceal himself."

One need only to ponder how exile and uncovered are etymologically linked to see how the concept can be a meaningful term as it pertains to the spiritual journey of an individual. In what sense is liminal experience, found in a person's exile from his comfortable or familiar surroundings, an exposure of the self to the transforming power of God? How is the exposure of the self to an unknown setting and environment exposing the essence of an individual or people? *Golah* is translated as "uncovered" in Leviticus chapters 18 and 20 to discuss prohibitions concerning impure sexual relationships between relatives. So does the act of uncovering through sexual intimacy relate to the intimacy of an individual or group in exile?

While the Hebrew word seems to emphasize the vulnerability of the individual in exile, the Greek word for exile seems to emphasize both the exile's temporary nature, and the otherness of the individual who is in a period of exile. The Greek word for exile, *parepidemos*, appears only six times in the New Testament – three of those in 1 Peter (Acts 7:29, 7:43; 1 Peter 1:1, 1:17, 2:11; Hebrews 11:13). In most cases where *parepidemos* is used the word has a clear political and social undertone. The individuals addressed are not to be influenced by the larger culture surrounding them. One's citizenship and community is no longer to be found in the immediate context of the state or of one's family. *The Theological Dictionary of the New Testament* states that in 1 Peter, "Christians are presented as men who have no country of their own on this earth; they are simply temporary residents" (Grundmann, *TDNT*, vol. 2 p. 65). The emphasis in 1 Peter is the transitory nature of the exiles' circumstances (Grundmann, vol. 2 p. 64). In his commentary on 1 Peter John Elliott writes, "The substantive *parepidemos* and its verb *parepidemeo* are used most often of the temporary visitor, the transient stranger who, as traveler passing through, has no intention or opportunity to establish permanent residence" (Elliott, *1 Peter*, 458). Hebrews 11:13 is the lone exception as regards the emphasis on the physical or socio-political nature of exile. Rather, the word is interpreted in light of the exiles' heavenly home. It is here that "exile" is allegorized and imbued with spiritual meaning. The author of Hebrews writes, "These all died in faith, not having received the things promised, but having seen them and greeted them from afar, and having acknowledged that they were strangers and exiles on the earth" (11:13). It is important also to take note of Ephesians 2:19 where, although *parepidemos* is not used by Paul, the concept is still expressed. "So then you are no longer strangers and aliens, but you are fellow citizens with the saints and members of the household of God."

Jeremiah 29

In Jeremiah 29:1-23 the prophet addresses those who have been carried away into exile and are looking forward to a quick return. It is written from Jerusalem to those in Babylon. Walter Brueggemann describes the context in which Jeremiah wrote and lived: "Jeremiah lived in a time of turmoil. He believed it was a time of dying. He envisioned the death of a culture, a society, a tradition" (Brueggemann, *Hopeful Imagination*, p. 32). His message was not the one the exiles were hoping to hear from the prophet. The exile would last 70 years, not the two or three years false prophets had told them. According to Jeremiah the exiles could expect three things in this 70-year period. First, it would not be devoid of God's presence. God would not only hear them in the present circumstances but, when the 70 years was over, he would move to restore the land to those taken into captivity. Second, the 70 years would be transformative. It was Jeremiah's conviction that God would work something new in the midst of the loss and sorrow. "For I know the plans I have for you, declares the Lord, plans for welfare and not for evil, to give you a future and a hope"

(Jeremiah 29:11). This transformation is characterized by a spiritual renewal, thus they would "face the exile, where God will meet this people afresh, perhaps with manna" (*Hopeful Imagination*, p. 31). Brueggemann emphasizes this point: "The six verbs in 1:10 concern losing the old world and receiving a new world; they are about relinquishing and receiving.... The verse (1:10) authorizes a fundamental displacement and discontinuity which the prophet must bring to speech" (*Hopeful Imagination*, p. 19). Third, there was work to be done in the interim. Simply because the exiles were disposed from the land did not mean they could remain idle and waste away. The 70 years were not without the continuity of family or civil responsibilities. Jeremiah encouraged his readers to continue to have families and give their children in marriage (Jeremiah 29:6). As the *New Century Bible Commentary* states: "The advice to build houses implies a certain freedom and opportunity" (Jones, p. 363). The exiles were to look after their own welfare, taking steps to feed themselves by planting gardens and working. Most interestingly, they were to look after the welfare of those who brought them into captivity. "But seek the welfare of the city where I have sent you into exile, and pray to the Lord on its behalf, for in its welfare you will find your welfare" (Jeremiah 29:7).

Jeremiah's instructions appear counterintuitive to individuals caught in their own personal times of exile. Ask any college student and the vast majority of them will have their eyes firmly fixed on moving toward "the real world." Neither would one in the midst of unemployment consider it his first priority to seek the welfare of those around him. Liminality is not a time of rest, or idleness. Indeed, from Jeremiah's account in Chapter 29, there is a sense that even in exile and displacement there is work to be done. Secondly, exile need not be a place where God is absent. It is clear from Jeremiah's account that God is present even in times where we would naturally assume his absence.

TWO NEW TESTAMENT EXAMPLES

The previous Old Testament passage considered exile in the context of the historical reality of the Babylonian captivity. First

Peter, on the other hand, addresses a group of people caught in an exile that is spiritual in nature. Peter describes his audience as exiles, with a sense of warmth and hope. He explicitly draws a comparison between Israel's experience and his readers' current circumstances. "The epistle appears to be a circular letter (1:1) addressed largely to Gentile Christians (1:14,18) who are metaphorically identified with Israel in exile" (Childs, *Biblical Theology of the Old and New Testaments*, p. 299). John Elliott writes, "The complete message of this letter becomes clear: Christian believers are strangers and without a home in society and indeed should remain so; for in the [house] of God [this exiled] society have found a home for the homeless" (Elliott, *1 Peter*, p. 482). In 1 and 2 Peter "exile is actually a spiritual designation for Christians away from their heavenly home" (Watson, *First and Second Peter*, p. 34).

This is not to say, however, that Peter takes lightly the physical or political circumstances of his audience. Elliott writes, "The constant perspective of this document is social not cosmological, and in this context ... describes a condition of social, not cosmological, estrangement" (*1 Peter*, p. 481). Neither is Peter's focus a matter of being so heavenly minded that he is no earthly good. Peter, Martin argues, "does not focus undue attention upon the past beginning or future destination of their journey. Rather, his concern is with their present travel between these two points" (Martin, *Metaphor and Composition in 1 Peter*, p. 155). Peter is also pointing to the historical context of the patriarchs, as Elliott states: "The entire phrase in which these two terms are combined here was undoubtedly inspired by Gen 23:4 LXX, the only other occurrence of this precise phrase in the ancient Greek literature prior to 1 Peter" (*1 Peter*, p. 477). Peter does not have only a spiritual reality in mind when speaking of his readers as aliens and foreigners; indeed, as another commentator states, the exhortation has practical consequences: "aliens as guests ... explains the two exhortations in this passage [1 Peter 2:13].... Together they form a balanced statement of the duties of aliens who are treated as guests" (*Metaphor and Composition*, pp. 196-197). Thus, just as in Jeremiah 29, Peter exhorts his audience in Chapter 2:13-15 to seek the general welfare of those around them.

> Be subject for the Lord's sake to every human institution, whether it be to the emperor as supreme, or to governors as sent by him to punish those who do evil and to praise those who do good. For this is the will of God, that by doing good you should put to silence the ignorance of foolish people.

So Peter's letter helps us consider how liminality requires a presence of mind in the present uncomfortable experience. Peter goes further, challenging the individual toward perseverance and obedience, encouraging his audience to trust in God's deliverance in the midst of circumstance not in the individual's control. As John Calvin said (in respect to another exilic passage, Ezekiel 12): "Even if we accomplish nothing through our labor, still God desires obedience" (Beckwith, *Ezekiel, Daniel*, p. 64).

A second New Testament example of the paradoxical nature of exile is found in the life of John the Divine. Like the exiles in Babylon, John finds himself forcefully removed from his home and ministry activity and exiled to a prison island off the coast of Asia Minor. It is there on the island, removed from his ministry, that he begins his work as the New Testament's strongest prophetic voice. On the island he receives "The revelation from Jesus Christ, which God gave him to show his servants what must soon take place"(Revelation 1:1). Also characteristic of exile is the type of creative and unique work John accomplishes in his time on the island. Biblical scholars have often noted the drastically different style and focus in the writings of John as compared other writers in the New Testament.

PSALM 137

So far we have examined Jeremiah 29 and 1Peter which provide insight into exile as a metaphor for liminality. They are texts whose authors write to those who are in the midst of the experience of exile. The next Scripture to be examined, Psalm 137, is written from the first-hand experience of exile. "The psalm appears to have been composed in the early part of the sixth century. The poet may have witnessed the events he recalls, or he may have belonged to the rising second generation of the exile (587-??? BCE)" (Terrien, *The Psalms*, p. 867). The psalm gives the reader a window into the experience itself. John Goldingay summarizes the psalm as follows:

> If there is a movement within the psalm, it rather starts with denial and a breakdown in relationship, and moves to recognition and communication. The beginning is aware of grief and abuse, but the community talks only to itself about it. In the last part it at last addresses God, but in doing so it also comes to express the longing in its heart concerning Jerusalem and concerning itself. (Goldingay, *Psalms*, v. 3, p. 611)

Thus Goldingay in his own words describes the sequence of liminal experience, from comfortableness, to confusion, and finally to a new experience of normal. Goldingay notes that the psalm does not merely record spiritual quagmire but highlights the complexity of the exilic experience: "The psalm is thus not merely an exercise in the movement between orientation, disorientation, and renewed orientation" (Goldingay, v. 3, p. 612).

Psalm 137 provides the reader with emotional insight into the exile experience. What is often lost in both the metaphor of exile and in the practical reality of exile is the emotional toll it takes on the individual. Even if it is considered as an all-around positive experience, say for example, in the lives of Ruth and Naomi, it is not one that can be gone through without emotional consequences.

The Psalms are the emotional touchstones of Scripture; they express depth of love for the creator God as well as anguish at his absence. James Montgomery Boice places Psalm 137 in its context: "We remember that in this final section of the Psalter (Psalm 135-150) we are dealing with psalms of praise. Here is a psalm that admits to a time and place where such praise was emotionally impossible. Moreover, along with the pathos of the opening stanza there is a harsh, angry outburst at the end...." (Boice, *Psalms*, p. 1188). In an article by John Patton he compares the psalm with our present culture: "Psalm 137 helps identify some of the fractures confronting us in today's world. I speak here of four of them (1) the fracture of oppression; (2) the fracture of homelessness; (3) the fracture of rage; and (4) the fracture of faith" (Patton, "Pastoral Ministry in a Fractured World," pp. 27). Or, as Marti Steussey argues, Psalm 137 is a response to trauma. The psalm "illustrates much that is common about human responses to trauma. Exposure to things that no human being should have to experience changes us. Many victims, including apparently this psalmist, feel a painful sense of shame and humiliation: 'for there...our tormenters asked for mirth'" (Steussy, "On Being Broken," pp. 33).

One can clearly see the structural movement of Psalm 137 from mourning, to despair, and then lastly to anger – anger which contains a call for justice. The first three verses of the psalm are characterized by grief and sorrow. They provide the setting as well as what one might consider the plot of the psalm.

> By the waters of Babylon,
> there we sat down and wept,
> when we remembered Zion.
>
> On the willows there
> we hung up our lyres.
>
> For there our captors
> required of us songs,
> and our tormentors, mirth, saying,
> "Sing us one of the songs of Zion!"
> (Psalm 137:1-3 ESV)

Goldingay compares the psalm with Isaiah, "The words … recall the way Isaiah 40:27 has the prophet talking about God rather than talking to God (Exodus 2:23). Thus they may be more an expression of religious depression" (*Psalms*, v. 3, p. 603). Goldingay in his commentary on the psalm has a contrasting view. "People's actual and proper attitude toward Babylon and Zion is weeping. Exiles usually grieve as they miss their homeland, though they may adjust" (*Psalms*, v. 3, 603). Goldingay also comments, "Perhaps v. 1 presupposes that people are consciously sitting before God and consciously weeping before God for their affliction and their waywardness" (*Psalms*, v. 3, 603).

Verses 4-6 are characterized by despair and longing for the remembered home.

> How shall we sing the Lord's song in a foreign land?
>
> If I forget you, O Jerusalem,
> let my right hand forget its skill!
>
> Let my tongue stick to the roof of my mouth,
> if I do not remember you,
> if I do not set Jerusalem
> above my highest joy! (Psalm 137:4-6 ESV)

Memory plays an incredibly important part in this psalm. The exiles long for what they once had – even as they look forward to the day when everything would be put right. As Walter Brueggemann states, "If we do not experience the pain, rage, and dis-ease that goes with such disequilibrium, we may be missing out on our call" (Brueggemann, *Hopeful Imagination*, 23).

Eventually this grief and despair turns to anger. The anger displayed by the psalmist is also a call for justice. Significantly absent from this call is the psalmist taking or wishing to take justice into his own hands. As disturbing as the imprecation might at first seem, Goldingay notes: "So now denial and a failure to communicate with YHWH has given way to communication with YHWH and an owning of their pain and longing." The Psalmist calls out to God, "Remember, O Lord," as if to say, "act in accordance with your own decrees."

> Remember, O Lord, against the Edomites
> the day of Jerusalem,

how they said, "Lay it bare, lay it bare,
down to its foundations!"

O daughter of Babylon, doomed to be destroyed,
blessed shall he be who repays you
with what you have done to us!

Blessed shall he be who takes your little ones
and dashes them against the rock! (Psalm 137:7-9 ESV)

John Patton does a marvelous job of noting the significant reality the Psalmist expresses. It is worth quoting at length:

> It is important here to recognize the difference between anger and rage, a difference that is more than just one of degree. Anger is a response to a particular verbal or physical injury. Rage is a response to what is perceived as an attack upon who I am – or against my whole family or nation. It is not specific but directed toward all who are seen as having power, as, for example, in the psalm where the rage is expressed against the whole new generation of oppressors. Old Testament scholar Walter Brueggemann has reminded us that the rage in the psalm is expressed in a prayer, not in action. God knows and accepts our rage and helps us contain it, but it cannot be overcome simply by being expressed, even in prayer. Rage must be restrained, prevented from leading to destructive action, and gradually overcome by a relationship that diminishes the feeling of being degraded or ultimately unimportant. (p. 28).

This call for justice in the midst of anger raises a number of important questions. For example, how do our emotions interact with and work with our sense of God's sovereignty? How might we express our anger justly? Or, to put it another way, how might anger be called upon to reaffirm our relationship with God?

APPLICATION AND IMPLICATION

Exile, despite its many hardships, is not without purpose or reward. From the three passages discussed above there are at least eight areas where exile provides significant insight into the lived faith of a Christian believer. First, exile brings about a greater or renewed revelation of God. Second, exile sharpens one's attention to issues concerning justice. Third, exile provides an opportunity to walk in obedience, and, fourth, to also walk in humility. Fifth, from exile comes a new and creative expression of an individual's or community's faith. This new expression of faith leads to a general transformation of the individual. This transformation of the individual also leads to an opportunity to witness to the nations. Finally, exile reaffirms the eschatological reality of a heavenly home.

New Revelation of God

As Lesquivit and Viard state, "By [the exile] God revealed to [Israel] his uncompromising holiness and his overwhelming faithfulness" (Lesquivit, "exile," *Dictionary of Biblical Theology*, p. 152). Douglas Jones notes in his commentary on the Jeremiah text: "Verses 11-14a are as revolutionary as they are unobtrusive. Jeremiah is affirming that when the exiles settle down to accept their banishment, they will find that their relationship with the LORD can be maintained, despite the absence of the props normally considered indispensable. 'Pray to me ... seek me and find me'" (*Jeremiah*, 1992, 365). Or, as Jones states, "to be an exile is still to be a person to whom the LORD may reveal himself."

Justice

One of the major themes within Psalm 137 is justice. "In a situation of mistreatment, an alien's only hope lay in his/her appeal to a higher authority" (Martin, 198). The exiles are forced to wrestle with not only their own sin and disobedience, but the reality that the world system is not just. The exiles of Psalm 137 are forced to seek justice in the living God. "Not all of the suffering caused by exile can be explained as judgment deserved, and the judgment wrought in exile does not equitably fall only on those who deserve it" (Jones, "Speaking to the Exiles," pp. 193).

Obedience and Humility

In light of God's ultimate adjudication of justice, the exile is to live a life of obedience and humility. As Martin describes concerning 1 Peter, "In fact, the entire paraenesis of the letter-body is designed to explicate the conduct or course of life appropriate for the eschatological travelers." (*Metaphor*, p. 155). Further on in his commentary Martin adds, "In addition to controlling their desires, guests were expected to submit or give way to their hosts since they had no claim to any rights" (*Metaphor*, 197). As the Lesquivit states, "From this time on, a humble confession of sins will become habitual in Israel (Jeremiah 31:19; Ezra 9:6; Nehemiah 1:6, 9,16,26; Daniel 9:5); the exile had become something like a 'negative theophany,' an unprecedented revelation of the holiness of God and of his detestation of evil" ("exile").

Creativity

The lessons learned in exile are not simply a matter of discipline and coping with difficult circumstance. Exile and the suffering inherent in it lead to an explosion of creativity. Victor Eldridge writes, "Exile did not lead Jews in the Old Testament to abandon faith or to settle for abdicating despair, nor to retreat to privatistic religion. On the contrary, exile evoked the most brilliant literature and the most daring articulation in the Old Testament" (Smith-Christopher, *A Biblical Theology of Exile*, 13). Brueggemann states this creative energy in the exilic prophets by saying, "Von Rad has seen that these three poets [Isaiah, Jeremiah and Ezekiel], more than any others, do not base their appeal on the continuing power of the old tradition but in fact enunciate new actions of God that are discontinuous with the old tradition" (*Hopeful Imagination*, p. 2).

Transformation and Mission

This creativity leads to two practical results: transformation and mission. From the fertile soil of trust and humility, the individual or the community is transformed. As Walter Brueggemann describes the Babylonian exile, it is a "story of newness acquired the hard way" (*Hopeful Imagination*, p. 33). Barry Jones writes, "In Jeremiah 29:13 one finds another description of seeking Yahweh with one's whole heart as a spiritual transformation that will emerge out of the exilic experience. The theme of a new covenant marked by inner spiritual transformation is repeated in Jeremiah 31:31-33" (Jones, "Speaking to the Exiles," pp. 177-200). He continues, "Several texts in Jeremiah reflect the belief that judgment now accomplished could give way to hope for the future. The exile of 587 marked not only an end but also a beginning" ("Speaking to the Exiles," pp. 177-200).

The other practical result of this creative environment is an individual or community being a witness to the greater population. "Peter does not call them to withdraw [but wishes them to engage] with society in the mode that might be expected of foreigners who wish to maintain their identity of origin" (Jobes, *1 Peter*, p. 40). This impetus to witness to the larger world is also in Jeremiah. "A final theme of Jeremiah that has ramifications for twenty-first century congregations is the theme of exile as an impetus to renewed mission. This theme is suggested in the language of Jeremiah 29:4 and 7" ("Speaking to the Exiles," pp. 177-200).

Eschatological Vision

Scripture reaffirms that exile ends and the believer will find himself or herself in an eschatological and heavenly home. "First Peter has taken over the conception of the diaspora as a journey in order to describe the existence of his readers as the wandering people of God on an eschatological journey" (Martin, 154). As fruitful or transformative as exile can be, exile is not the final state of the elect of God. This can be thought of in two ways. First, one needs only to examine other biblical figures (Nehemiah for example) and notice how many of them begin their full ministry and kingdom work after their return from exile. (See the life of Paul or Moses as two clear examples of this pattern.) Boice says, "[The exiles] nevertheless did not break their harps in pieces or throw them in the stream. Instead they hung them on the poplars, presumably saving them for what would surely be a better day" (Boice, p. 1189). A second consideration is the larger view that all of life is exile and death is the beginning of true life. One might seriously consider that the message of Revelation is the return of Christ, who will usher in the real work of the elect.

In conclusion, the metaphor of exile provides both practical pastoral guidance and reasons to hope in the midst of exilic liminal experience. On the one hand, exile tells us that the liminal experience must be obediently lived through with humility. The very word for exile reveals the process as one in which the individual is exposed to God's judgment and grace. On the other hand, the liminal experience must be an active engagement. The individual believer should not passively wait for God to remove him or her from the liminal experience. Rather, as the individual person is transformed – he or she becomes an active witness of God's purpose and sovereign justice. What Shimon Bakon says of the Jewish nation may equally be said of the individual,

> "Jews in exile, cleansed of idolatry, remained steadfast in their Jewish identity, and were yearning for a return. It can be stated with near certainty that the 124 or 136 years, intervening between 722 to 598 or 586, were decisive for Judaism. These were the years of the great prophets: Hosea and Amos, Isaiah and Micah, Jeremiah and Ezekiel. Their messages, while not effective for their contemporaries, eventually and cumulatively had their impact and penetrated the very being of the Jewish soul " (Bakon, "Exile and Return," pp. 101-108).

For the Christian, the process through exile transforms the individual through displacement and mourning into active missional engagement for the world.

CHAPTER 3

HOLY SATURDAY

The third metaphor for liminality poses unique difficulties for both the scholar and the growing believer. The first of these problems is terminology. What word do we use to label this unique metaphor of liminality? Tomb, death, and Holy Saturday all are viable candidates. Each of these terms helps us focus on the dark reality of liminal time. Holy Saturday highlights the irony of the metaphor. The Saturday following Christ's death is laced between its darkness and its sacred character. The second difficulty is the biblical silence on the issue. Very little is written concerning the historical events or theological meaning found in the events of that Saturday. There is no New Testament author to provide a theological interpretation of Holy Saturday. In addition to this there is only one Old Testament parallel to Holy Saturday, Jonah's captivity in the belly of the whale. However, this account is itself a metaphor for death and resurrection.

Despite the difficulties stated above, this particular metaphor for liminal space has unique qualities that beckon a further and closer examination. Shelly Rambo states, "Holy Saturday narrates a more indecipherable time and place in which death and life are being brought into a unique relationship" (Rambo, *Spirit and Trauma*, p. 46). First, since the metaphor encompasses a wide range of ideas, it can lead to extraordinary connections. For example, in his commentary on Lamentations, Robin Parry states, "Lamentations then is to the exile and restoration of Israel what Holy Saturday is to the cross and resurrection of Christ" (Parry, *Lamentations*, p. 173).

Second, death as a liminal concept is the most missional and other-centered of the three metaphors. Unlike exile and wilderness which are chiefly characterized by the purification and formation of a person or group, the metaphor of the tomb is rich with the notion of proclamation and mission. As we will see, Jonah's resurrection experience leads to the missional proclamation of repentance to Nineveh. Nikoloas Vassiliadis suggests Christ's death experience was a means for proclaiming God's sovereignty: "The Lord descended into Hades as a powerful besieger of death, in order to complete the predetermined divine plan of our salvation" (Vassiliadis, *The Mystery of Death*, p. 183). The tomb is to *missio dei* as wilderness and exile are to sanctification. Third, the concept places a greater focus on power and strength: "The victory of the God-man over death and hades began precisely at the point where His enemies thought they had defeated him" (Vassiliadis, p. 163).

This chapter will be divided differently from the preceding two chapters. The initial section will contain an examination of Psalm 88. This is an individual whose lament against God – perceived as the psalmist's enemy – goes unanswered. The middle section of the chapter is an investigation of the New Testament references to Christ's death and experience during Holy Saturday. The New Testament passages seem to be inter-canonically responding to the psalmist's questions. The last section of the chapter will explore Jonah's great cry from within the belly of the whale found in Jonah 2. Jonah's experiences both there and in the rest of the narrative seem to place Psalm 88 and the 1 Peter verses into a seamless complete picture of the two passages previously discussed. The paper will conclude by drawing both missional implications and baptismal insights for the individual who seeks to "take up his cross daily and follow me" (Luke 9:23).

PSALM 88

Psalm 88 is one of the bleakest psalms in the entire Psalter. In the 1979 Book of Common Prayer written for the Episcopal Church, Psalm 88 is one of the psalms used in the daily office on Holy Saturday. In Psalm 88 the author cries out to God, whom he is not entirely sure is willing to hear him (Illman, "Psalm 88: a Lamentation without Answer," p. 120). He feels that he has been abandoned by God and left to suffer alone in his agony. John Goldingay in his commentary on Psalm 88 notes that rather than closure, the psalm simply trails off. The psalmist is exhausted by his repeated cries to God with a petition God is not interested in hearing (Goldingay, v2, p. 644).

Psalm 88 repeats a single plea, starting with verse 2, "Let my prayer come before you; incline your ear to my cry!" This is a plea to simply be heard, listened to, and acknowledged by the God who has brought the psalmist to this point in his life. The Psalmist repeats this plea three times in the psalm: 1-2, 9b-c, and finally again in verse 13 (Goldingay, v2, p. 644). The repetition of the plea forms one half of the basic structure of the psalm. The second part of the structure is the chiastic form that begins after verse 4, placing verse 11-13 at the climax of the psalm. This, as noted above, contains the third repeated plea to God to listen to the complainant.

Why is the psalmist begging God to listen to him? The most direct answer is found in verse 3: "For my soul is full of troubles, and my life draws near to Sheol." The psalmist is at the brink of death. Indeed most interpreters believe that there is some type of physical cause of the author's distress. From his youth (verse 15) he has faced a chronic illness of some type (Illman, *Obadiah, Jonah, Micah*, pp. 112-120). However, to read the psalmist's complaint as merely about physical suffering is to miss the anguish in the author's words. The central emotions of the psalm are abandonment and loneliness. His friends and loved ones have departed. They have been made to look on him with scorn (vv. 8, 18). Unlike many other lamentations in the psalms, his enemies are not responsible. Indeed, enemies are remarkably absent from his account. Finally, unlike other psalms in the canon, there is no mention of the psalmist's guilt. While he may – as theologically he must – be guilty of sin in his life, sin is not the cause of his current troubles. His feelings of being brought to the point of death and exhaustion are not the result of disobedience as with Israel's exile into Babylon.

The psalmist feels it is God who is ultimately responsible for his plight. The psalm is a long complaint, telling God just exactly how the psalmist feels in his current condition. As Illman states, "The psalmist sees himself as standing under the wrath of God (8a. 17a), who has turned away from him (15b). God has rejected him (15a) and placed him far away from himself (7) in deep misery (8,

9)" ("Psalm 88," pp. 112-120). It is necessary to pause and note that as with the other liminal metaphors we have encountered, God is seen as ultimately responsible for the condition of the one caught in liminal space.

As mentioned above, the psalm ends with questions, not answers. God does not respond to the cries of the psalmist, and the psalm figuratively and literally ends in "darkness." Here at this point in the discussion of liminality it seems wise to pause and address a critical danger. An individual in a liminal moment of his life will experience incredibly strong and dark emotions. One who counsels such a person, or a person who seeks to counsel himself or herself through such a period, must balance two biblical tensions. On the one hand, the emotions are real, the feelings of abandonment and confusion are real. To deny these feelings is to run the risk of disassociating oneself from one's own life. On the other hand, despite the darkness, as has been recounted already and will be discussed further, God's truth extends above and beyond our emotional states through periods of death, wilderness, and exile. A biblical balance must be sought between the theological unchanging truth of God's goodness and the existential momentary crises brought on by difficult circumstances. So what then can we turn to as the fulcrum on which these two realities must be balanced? The answer is Christ. Without being glib or cute, but in earnest seriousness, Christ's own experiences in death finally give answer to the psalmist's unanswered cry.

1 PETER AND HOLY SATURDAY

It is not at all surprising that 1 Peter 3:19 and 1 Peter 4:6 are two of the most controversial verses in all of Scripture. Interpretative questions abound. What does it mean that Christ proclaimed? Whom in fact did he proclaim to? What is meant by prison? Where exactly is this prison located? It is clearly understood by most scholars today that some of the original meaning for the original audience has been lost, and this has, unlike other passages, caused a serious defect in our understanding of this passage. Peter seems to depend on his audience to provide a context for what he is arguing for even as those in the present audience fail to make the connection (von Balthasar, *Mysterium Paschale*, p. 157). The original biblical audience was much more familiar with stories of people descending to the dead and their eventual return and may have understood more clearly what Peter meant (Kittel, *TDNT*, v6, 568).

Regardless of the nuanced meaning for the original audience, most scholars believe these two verses refer to Christ's descent into hell and his proclaiming victory over demonic beings, entrapped there since the times of Noah (Schreiner, *1, 2 Peter, Jude*, p. 182). However, one should not discount the well-established historical teaching of the Church. Joel Green writes, "From the early second century on, Peter was widely regarded as referring to Christ's descent into Hades in order that he might (1) share fully the fate of humanity, (2) conquer Death or Hades (or both), (3) rescue the righteous dead, and/or (4) proclaim salvation to the dead" (Green, *1 Peter*, 128). The historical consensus and the modern agreement to the meaning of the text do not negate one another. Whatever the details and exact historical reality of Christ's activities on Holy Saturday, there remain two startling realities.

First is the fact that Christ died and traveled to a location where spirits, and humans (as evidenced by 4:6) have been locked away. Indeed as von Balthasar states, Christ's descent is "the ultimate solidarity … the final point and the goal of that first 'descent,' so clearly described in the scriptures" (von Balthasar, 164). One might cautiously state that Christ is no more human than when he identifies with humanity's punishment for sin, and by implication this includes our fated resting place in hell. As the author of Psalm 88 cries out for God to hear him and seemingly is ignored, Christ himself finds that he has taken the same course. Both Christ and the psalmist find themselves powerless to avoid death and its consequences. "Deprived of all strength and all vitality (Isaiah 14:10) the dead are called *refa'aim,* the powerless ones.... They dwell in the country of forgetfulness (Psalm 88:13)" (*Mysterium Paschale*, 164).

Second, and paradoxically, Christ enters hell not as victim or a defeated foe, but as victor. His mission in hell is to stake his claim to the underworld and those who reside there. As Paul declares in Romans 14:9, "For to this end Christ died and lived again, that he might be Lord both of the dead and of the living. The word "proclaim" in 3:19 is most often understood as meaning "to publicly announce religious truths and principles while urging acceptance and compliance" (Louw, v1, 41). Thus, as I. Howard Marshall states, "Christ made proclamation to the evil powers, announcing his victory on the cross and confirming their defeat. They are now subject to him (3:22) and those who are persecuted need not be afraid of the evil spiritual powers who inspire their persecutors. Christ is Lord! Hallelujah!" (Marshall, *1 Peter*, p. 138).

JONAH 2

Psalm 88 reflects the downward descent and despair of a person caught in the throes of death. First Peter tells us that no one less than God himself has identified with these very feelings. Christ, through the passage of 1 Peter, has also proclaimed his sovereign control over these moments of terror. So there remains the question: Where do we see the despair of Psalm 88 and the solidarity and power of 1 Peter placed together in the biblical narrative? The answer is found in Jonah Chapter 2.

As with Psalm 88, Jonah 2 relies on water images to help convey deep trouble and nearness to death. Water appears no less than seven times in the chapter; Psalm 88 uses the same image twice. In both cases water is used to describe overwhelmed feelings. When Jonah calls out from the belly of the whale he is expressing his removal and utmost distance from God (Jenson, 65). Yet, even as Jonah feels removed, his words in verse one, calling out to "the Lord his God" indicate a close relationship with the one who placed Jonah in the whale's innards (Jenson, 62). Jonah's circumstances serve God's plans and desires, not Jonah's. In all three passages, the main character has been brought to Sheol, whether figuratively or literally.

Unlike Psalm 88, Jonah does not end on this note of despair. Jonah understands that God is responsible for bringing him from one danger, the boat in the midst of the storm, into the remote darkness of the belly of the whale. And Jonah's prayer is a confident assertion that God will redeem Jonah out of his present circumstances. His prayer quickly moves from despair to trust. Jonah moves from third person testimony of what God has done to second person thanksgiving. Jonah understands and is secure in the knowledge that his salvation is certain. "With the natural man arises first defiance, then despair: with the redeemed man strength is realized out of despair by the power of the spirit. The declarations of faith are all paradoxes and contrasts. Because I suffer, I shall be glorified" (Lange, *Jonah*, p. 28).

After Jonah's experience in the whale he is now empowered with a renewed sense of faith to carry out his original charge by God – to preach to the city of Nineveh. What he was unwilling to do before his liminal experience in the belly of a whale, he is now able to carry out. Just like the Prodigal Son of the New Testament, Jonah is able to become the prophet he was intended to be at the beginning (Smith, *Amos, Obadiah, Jonah*, p. 250).

CONCLUSION

We may now make some general applications as regards death as a metaphor for liminality. First, we can gain a new appreciation for baptism. Sandwiched between 1 Peter 3:19 and 1 Peter 4:6 is 3:21, concerning the sacrament of baptism: "Baptism, which corresponds to this, now saves you, not as a removal of dirt from the body but as an appeal to God for a good conscience, through the resurrection of Jesus Christ." Or as Romans 6:4 states, "We were buried therefore with him by baptism into death, in order that, just as Christ was raised from the dead by the glory of the Father, we too might walk in newness of life." The extensive use of water in the other two passages discussed above make a case for considering baptism as the sacrament of liminality. Baptism moves one from death in one's sins, to Christ's claim of power over the individual, and finally a movement up and out toward a new life and a commissioning into the proclamation of the gospel. "… for Peter, the word 'baptism' symbolically represents the whole process

by which the gospel comes to people and they accept it in faith"
(Marshall, *1 Peter*, 140).

Second, we can understand the liminal metaphor of death as
one that draws explicit attention to the community of those who
suffer. Liminal space as expressed in Psalm 88 can be an isolating
and lonely period of time. However, Christ has gone to the outer-
most lengths to identify with our suffering. Those in liminal space
are not unique: prophets, psalmists, even Christ himself have experienced this frightening time of death.

The third application is the reality of the power of Christ over
death and our painful circumstances. Christ has claimed victory
over evil and his triumphant proclamation to those in hell assures
those who follow him that even in the midst of our own suffering
Christ reigns as King. As I. Howard Marshall notes, persecution
and isolation raise the question of God's control over our circumstances (Marshall, p. 137). God's response is to provide his Son,
Jesus Christ, as a living reminder that in every human experience,
God reigns supreme.

Finally, death and Holy Saturday as a liminal metaphor place
a greater emphasis on the mission of God. Jonah runs away from
his calling to preach repentance to the city of Nineveh. However,
through his time in the belly of Sheol, he is made willing and
obedient to God's call. Jonah is empowered to carry out the task
placed before him. Likewise in 1 Peter we see Christ proclaim and
empower individuals for the gospel. Christ dies and is resurrected;
as a result his followers are empowered by the Holy Spirit to proclaim the good news. Indeed, as is made explicit in 1 Peter, Christ
proclaims the new reality of a means for man to be reconciled to
God through his death and suffering on the Cross, not to mention
his rule over even those in hell.

HISTORICAL-THEOLOGICAL
PERSPECTIVE

CHAPTER 4

AUGUSTINE

The description of liminality as a time of inner spiritual wrestling which brings about growth and maturity aptly characterizes the conversion experience of St. Augustine in his autobiography, *The Confessions of Saint Augustine.* Books one through nine present the slow process of his intellectual and spiritual conversion. *The Confessions* is the crowning achievement in what was a familiar genre of literature in the late Roman Empire. However, it also helped to highlight the growing changes within the church and Christianity in general. Peter Brown provides historical context for the life of Augustine: "By the time of Augustine, the Church had settled down in Roman Society. The Christian's enemy could no longer be placed outside him: they were inside, his sins and his doubts; and the climax of a man's life would not be martyrdom, but conversion from the perils of his own past" (Brown, *Augustine of Hippo*, 152).

Augustine presents the reader with a detailed account of his inner spiritual journey. This chapter looks at three aspects of Augustine's conversion process, which uncannily aligns with the pattern of liminal experiences already discussed in this work. First to be examined is the way Augustine describes his liminal experience. Second, we will examine where in Augustine's life this experience is taking place. Finally, we will ask, "What outcome(s) does liminal experience have in the life of Augustine?"

It will prove helpful if we quote at length the climax of Augustine's conversion/liminal experience. The long journey to Christian faith climaxes in Book 8 Chapter 11:

> Within myself I said: "Behold, let it be done now, now let
> it be done," and by those words I was already moving on to a
> decision. By then I had almost made it, and yet I did not make

it. Still, I did not slip back into my former ways, but close by
I stood my ground and regained my breath. Again I tried, and
I was but a little away from my goal, just a little away from it,
and I all but reached it and laid hold of it. I still hesitated to
die to death and to live to life, for the ingrown worse had more
power over me than the untried better. The nearer came that
moment in time when I was to become something different,
the greater terror did it strike into me. Yet it did not strike me
back, nor did it turn me away, but it held me in suspense....
I hesitated to tear myself away, and shake myself free of them,
and leap over to that place where I was called to be. (*Confessions*, p. 200).

James O'Donnell in his commentary on *The Confessions* notes
how this section of Augustine's book is unique and is set apart
from the larger whole. Book 8 of *The Confessions* parallels the book
of Romans. There are seven quotations from Romans in book 8.
Augustine's conversion appears in the crucial sequential order and
parallels Romans 7 (O'Donnell, 4). Romans 7:15 is arguably the
prime example of liminality in the Bible: "For I do not understand my own actions. For I do not do what I want, but I do the
very thing I hate." O'Donnell notes, "The comparative drought of
scripture echoes has the effect of emphasizing Augustine's self-con-
structed isolation (which he is about to surrender) and prepares for
the flood of them in the decisive paragraphs" (O'Donnell, *Augustine
Confessions*, p. 51).

Throughout *The Confessions*, Augustine uses a multitude of
words and images to describe the liminal experience. Many of these
describe physical symptoms, as in the above quote where he says,
"I hesitated to tear myself away" (*Confessions*, p. 200). He describes
these intense times as leaving him "breathless" or with "speechless
dread" (*Confessions*, p. 194). In earlier passages Augustine's description could be seen as a heightened, possibly even clinical state of
anxiety. "Therefore I raged, and sighed, and wept, and became dis-
traught, and there was for me neither rest nor reason" (*Confessions*,
p. 100). He openly describes himself as suffering "from a madness"
(*Confessions*, p. 195). It all leaves Augustine disoriented. "To myself

I became a great riddle, and [my soul] could answer me nothing" (*Confessions*, p. 98).

Similarly, the 20th-century theologian Henri Nouwen wrote of having a similar experience in his meditation on Rembrandt's great painting, *The Return of the Prodigal Son*: "I have tried so hard in the past to heal myself from my complaints and failed … and failed, until I came to the edge of complete emotional collapse and even physical exhaustion. I can only be healed from above, from where God reaches down" (Nouwen, *The Return of the Prodigal Son*, p. 76).

On other occasions, Augustine describes his experience more along the lines of a battle with himself: "… no one would stop the raging combat that I had entered into against myself" (*Confessions*, p. 195). Just paragraphs before the climatic conversion, Augustine writes, "Thus did my two wills, the one old, the other new, the first carnal, and the second spiritual, contend with one another, and by their conflict they laid waste my soul" (*Confessions*, p. 198). These liminal experiences are incredibly intense struggles. Sometimes Augustine compares the experience with death. For example, "There remained only speechless dread and my soul was fearful, as if of death itself, of being kept back from that flow of habit by which it was wasting away unto death" (*Confessions*, p. 194).

As this quote indicates, Augustine's struggle is both interior and spiritual. As he states in book 8, "I went into myself … did I not lash my soul" (*Confessions*, 194). From the climatic account of his conversion, he describes the struggle as taking place "Within myself" (*Confessions*, p. 200). And again the object of his wrestling is his own interior landscape: "To myself I became a great riddle, and I questioned my soul as to why it was sad and why it afflicted me so grievously, and it could answer me nothing" (*Confessions*, p. 98). Nouwen, more than 1,500 years later, would acknowledge, "I am called to enter not the inner sanctuary of my own being where God has chosen to dwell" (*Prodigal*, p. 18).

To what end is all this wrestling, combat and interior examination? In short, the suffering leads Augustine to new life: "I suffered from a madness that was to bring health, and I was in a death agony that was to bring life" (*Confessions*, p. 195). It was a struggle to be where he was called to be and to be brought from death to life, as his climatic conversion account describes: "I still hesitated to die to death and to live to life" (*Confessions*, p. 200). This struggle ultimately led not only to life but life with joy. "Everywhere a greater joy is preceded by a greater suffering" (Augustine, 186).

It should not come as a surprise to any reader that Augustine's liminal experiences are initiated and overseen by God himself. *The Confessions*, after all, is a joyful declaration of God's sovereign plan in the life of Augustine. Time and time again Augustine acknowledges God's sovereign plan in his life and the role God played in preparing him for useful service in his kingdom. He prays, "Being thus admonished to return to myself, under your leadership I entered into my inmost being. This I could do, for you became my helper" (Augustine, 170). Later Augustine writes, "You have called to me, and have cried out, and have shattered my deafness" (Augustine, 254). Ultimately the record of the liminal experiences in the process of his conversion are there to reinforce his thesis found in book one, chapter one, that, "our heart is restless until it rests in you" (*Confessions*, 43).

CHAPTER 5

JULIAN OF NORWICH

Julian of Norwich was an Anchorite nun, born most likely in 1342, who lived her life secluded in small rooms attached to the church in Norwich, England. Her *Revelation of Divine Love* is a complex and mystical narrative that recounts her visions of Christ's death on the Cross and in the process passes along advice to her fellow nuns on living the Christian life faithfully. Living a faithful life, one can easily speculate, was not an easy task, as Julian lived and wrote during the turbulent 14th century, a century which saw the Hundred Years War, the Babylonian Captivity of the Papacy (which saw as many as three different men claiming to be the pope) and the Black Death.[1] *The Revelation of Divine Love* exists in two forms. The first version is a shortened composition composed when she was 30, at or about the time she received the original vision (Ryan, 140). The second longer version was composed about 20 years later and demonstrates a long critical process of reflecting on the original vision.

Julian's writing is characterized by a personal and deeply felt sense of pain and loss. This is compounded by Julian's sense of longing for unity with Christ. In spite of this, Julian displays a compelling trust in God's sovereign plan for the believer's life. Further compounding the contradiction between deep feelings of longing and experiences of suffering are equally rich themes of joy and God's love for the saints. One does not expect the range of emotions in her writing nor does one expect the ease at which they lay side by side in her narrative. As Robin Ryan summarizes

---

1   For more on this time period see Barbra Tuchman's excellent work *A Distant Mirror*.

Barbara Wertheim Tuchman, *A Distant Mirror: The Calamitous 14th Century*, (1st trade ed. New York: Knopf, 1978).

Julian, "The appeal of her work is due, at least in part, to the fact that she integrates two contrasting experiences of human life and the search for God: a profound immersion in the mystery of sin and suffering on the one hand, and compelling insight into the joy and hope that God's love offers us on the other" (Ryan, p. 140).

One cannot go very far in reading Julian of Norwich before one is confronted with her vision of Christ's suffering. Julian's mystical visions gave her a "front row seat" as it were. In *Divine Love* Julian's mediations on these sufferings become a source of inspiration for her to bear under the suffering in her own life. As Ryan asserts, "Julian became convinced that contemplation of the suffering Christ was the most effective means of personal transformation, resulting in a more profound love of Christ. It was also the pathway to deepened insight into the mystery of God" (*Human Suffering*, 140). Just as Christ was left alone on the cross, abandoned and left to suffer by God the Father, Julian encourages her readers to abide and thrive in the midst of their own struggles. This theme of suffering and aloneness is established as early as the 10th chapter. Julian writes, "The soul … may do no more than seek, suffer and trust" (*Human Suffering*, 315). A few pages later she notes of her own experience, "I was turned and left to myself in heaviness, and weariness of my life, and irksomeness of myself, that scarcely I could have patience to live. There was no comfort nor none ease…." (Julian, *Revelations of Divine Love*, loc. 433). In Chapter 41 Julian uses images connected with physical illness and the desert to describe her experiences. Writing as if in the voice of God the Father and speaking directly to herself, she writes, "For in dryness and in barrenness, in sickness and in feebleness, then is thy prayer well-pleasant to me" (*Revelations*, loc. 1014).

In Julian's writings there is a strong sensation of longing. Indeed it appears from her writings as if longing is a natural and necessary component of the Christian life. "And of the virtue of this longing in Christ, we have to long again to Him: *without which no soul cometh to Heaven*. And this property of longing and thirst cometh of the endless Goodness of God" (*Revelations*, loc. 772-774, emphasis by author). Two items from this quote need to be especially emphasized. First, longing is tied to one's sanctification. One cannot find oneself whole without the process of longing after God. She states in another section of her writing, "[it is through] true longing toward God we are made worthy" (*Revelations*, loc. 954). Second, this longing, and we will see this as a motif in Julian's writing, originates out of God's goodness toward his children. One wonders if Peter's exilic longing was not in the back of her mind as she wrote concerning the believer's entering into the promised rest.

For Julian, longing for God's presence, and suffering through his absence or the arrows of this world, are almost always couched in the middle of God's sovereign plan. Suffering and longing do not exist outside of God's rule. For example, Julian states, "God willeth that we know that He keepeth us even alike secure in woe and in weal. And for profit of man's soul, a man is sometime *left to himself,* although sin is not always the cause" (*Revelations*, loc. 441). That is, she says, not all suffering and pain are the product of disobedience. The spiritual longing typical of the pilgrim, according to Julian, originates in God himself. God is in sovereign control, organizing the experience of the believer for the full glory of God himself. "Thus He hath ruth and compassion on us, and He hath longing to have us; but His wisdom and His love suffereth not the end to come till the best time" (*Revelations*, loc. 776). It is God's plan by which he organizes our lives, but it is a plan saturated with a deep love for the one God is directing. "But freely our Lord giveth when He will; and suffereth us [to be] in woe sometime. And both is one love" (*Revelations*, loc. 443). For as she states, "Pity in love keepeth us in the time of our need" (Julian, loc. 2037). And at the halfway mark of her narrative she states, in chapter 46, that we are "the soul led by love" (*Revelations*, loc. 1148).

In the writings of Julian, there are at least three clearly definable reasons for the suffering and longing each person must endure. As genuine as the pain is for the saint, it is all in due course of God's will to bring joy and fulfillment to the one God loves. The first reason for suffering is the bliss or joy the disciple encounters as a result: suffering "keep[s] and lead[s] into the fulness of joy" (*Revelations*, loc. 2101). Julian states, "The seeking ... pleaseth our

Lord, and the finding pleaseth the soul and fulfilleth it with joy" (*Revelations*, loc. 315). Moreover, something unique is imparted to the one who has experienced the suffering. "... for the time that He will suffer the soul to be in travail. It is God's will that we seek Him, to the beholding of Him, for by that He shall shew us Himself of His special grace when He will" (Julian, loc. 318). Or again, "[God] shall see that all the woe and tribulation that he hath done to them shall be turned to increase of their joy, without end" (*Revelations*, loc. 404). It is in fact a constant theme within *Revelations of Divine Love:* trial and suffering lead to joy. "Take now heed faithfully and trustingly, and at the last end thou shalt verily see it in fulness of joy. [God] would have us the more eased in our soul and [the more] set at peace in love – leaving the beholding of all troublous things that might keep us back from true enjoying of Him" (*Revelations*, loc. 795).

The second purpose of suffering and longing Julian identifies is that of worship. She points out that "the harder our pains have been with Him in His Cross, the more shall our worship be with Him in His kingdom" (Julian, Kindle, 570). She clarifies her belief stating "not that any evil is worshipful, but I say the sufferance of our Lord God is worshipful" (Julian, Kindle, 858-859). Pain will be turned into worship. "The other [reason to be shown Christ's passion] is for comfort in our pain: for He willeth that we perceive that it shall all be turned to worship and profit by virtue of His passion" (Julian, Kindle, 720-721).

Third, with suffering and longing comes a genuine union with God and knowledge of God. Julian writes, "Through learning in this little pain that we suffer here, we shall have an high endless knowledge of God which we could never have without that" (Julian, Kindle, 556). Pain, in Julian's thinking, is one of the tools, a means to a greater end: intimacy with the Almighty. It is from our difficult experiences that God will show us a much richer experience of his presence. "Therefore this is [God's] thirst and love-longing, to have us altogether whole in Him, to His bliss – as to my sight. For we be not now as fully whole in Him as we shall be" (Julian, loc. 760).

Julian pulls many of the contradictory strands together toward the end of her *Revelation of Divine Love*, stating:

> For His love maketh Him to long [for us]; His wisdom and His truth with His rightfulness maketh Him to suffer us [to be] here: and in this same manner [of longing and abiding] He willeth to see it in us. For this is our natural penance – and the highest, as to my sight. For this penance goeth never from us till what time that we be fulfilled, when we shall have Him to our meed. And therefore He willeth that we set our hearts in the Overpassing: that is to say, from the pain that we feel into the bliss that we trust. (*Revelations*, loc. 2190-2194).

Julian does the same thing in this section of her revelation just prior to the above quotation:

> And when that we be fallen, by frailty or blindness, then our courteous Lord toucheth us and stirreth us and calleth us; and then willeth He that we see our wretchedness and meekly be aware of it. But He willeth not that we abide thus, nor He willeth not that we busy us greatly about our accusing, nor He willeth not that we be wretched over our self; but He willeth that we hastily turn ourselves unto Him. (*Revelations*, loc. 2150).

What can we say about these dominate themes? Is there anything that might tie them together for a more definitive whole? How is it that she can hold onto joy and suffering with such seeming ease? One way to understand this contradiction is to see it through the lens of liminal experience. It is not the only meta-theme within her writing and certainly not the clearest touchstone within her deeply devotional work, however it is nonetheless a tool by which we can unify the extremes of her suffering and loneliness with her confidence in the love and joy to be found in a closer relationship with Christ.

There are three points for asserting that she is describing a liminal experience. One, notice that Julian does not ignore or deny the severity of suffering or the depth of her loneliness. She is not avoiding the uncomfortableness or tests of faith such experiences bring. Rather, she rides the rail between them, holding the uncomfortableness of suffering in one hand and the expected joy in the other. Two, this pain and suffering is nevertheless tied to a full trust in God's love and care. This is evidenced by the repeated back and forth of suffering and God's love, often within the very same sentence. Three, she recognizes that the joy and bliss she sees is still oftentimes an object in the far distant future. For example, she states, "I was learned that our soul shall never have rest till it cometh to Him, knowing that He is fulness of joy" (*Revelations*, loc. 673). Notice the tie in with Augustine's "Our hearts are restless until they rest in Thee."). At about the midpoint of her revelation she says, "we shall never have full rest till we see Him verily and clearly in heaven" (*Revelations*, loc. 1170).

In conclusion, much of Julian's witness to the crucifixion of Christ and the experience of loss and suffering are done in the larger context of God's sovereign plan and God's love for the believer. Like Augustine's *Confessions,* the narrative can be read on a number of levels. It is a work of theology, a meditation on the atonement, a devotional reflection of a nun's mystical visions ... and it can also be seen as something in between: A narrative of a believer's wrestling with the implication of suffering in her life and the love that has been demonstrated to be hers through the death of Christ on the cross.

CHAPTER 6

ST. JOHN OF THE CROSS

St. John of the Cross is the theologian most likely to come to mind when discussing the topic of liminality. His book, *The Dark Night of the Soul*, has become synonymous with the experience of testing and trial identified within this work as liminality. However, it will come as a surprise to many readers to find St. John of the Cross expressing, more clearly than any of the other authors in the second part of this study, the intimate, joyful nature of the liminal experience. Throughout his work, St. John of the Cross ties the dark night of the soul to an outcome that is meant to bring on a spiritual union between believer and almighty God. Indeed, the dark night of the soul is initiated by a loving God who sets out to bring about a greater connection and peace between him and his beloved children.

There is reasonable evidence to support the claim of St. John of the Cross as the liminal theologian *par excellence*. For example, Peter Tyler summarizes St. John's understanding of the dark night as "The place where we encounter our own nothingness and insecurity…. It is a place of paradox" (Tyler, "St. John of the Cross," pp. 301-310). St. John of the Cross himself compares the dark night with the wilderness experience of the Exodus. "These souls whom God is beginning to lead through these solitary places of the wilderness are like to the children of Israel" (St. John of the Cross, *Ascent of Mount Carmel, Dark Night of the Soul, & A Spiritual Canticle of the Soul and Bridegroom Christ*, p. 416). Indeed St. John writes in the *Dark Night* describing many of the characteristics of liminality as have already been discussed.

This dark night is an inflowing of God into the soul, which purges it from its ignorances and imperfections…. Hearing God secretly teaches the soul and instructs it in perfection of love without its doing anything, or understanding of what manner is this infused contemplation. Inasmuch as it is the loving wisdom of God, God produces striking effects in the soul for, by purging and illumining it, He prepares it for the union of love with God. (*Ascents*, p. 444).

From the above excerpt from St. John of the Cross, one clearly discerns several key liminal hallmarks. For a start, just as Peter Tyler highlighted, the dark night is characterized by the paradoxical. It is a difficult time of immense blessing. Second, God's presence is felt as a painful and difficult purge. Third, this experience is meant to cleanse an individual, making him or her a vessel of God's presence. Fourth, God is directing and leading the individual in the process of the dark night. Finally, St. John emphasizes the intimacy between God and the pilgrim, the ultimate outcome of the dark night.

St. John of the Cross was born June 24, 1542 in Fontiveros, a village forty miles due east of Salamanca in the north-west part of Spain (Tyler, pp. 301-310). He was the youngest of three sons and was fortunate enough to be noticed by religious leaders in his community. These leaders provided the financial support and educational opportunities which eventually allowed him to study at the local university. After his studies at the university, at the age of 21, he entered the Carmelite order of monks at Medina del Campo. A few years later St. John was ordained as a priest in the Roman Catholic Church. It was also at this time that St. John encountered Theresa of Avila, who encouraged him to aid her in reforming the Carmelite order (Perrin, "The Unique Contribution of John of the Cross to the Western Mystical Tradition," pp. 199-230). From these beginnings he would rise through the ranks first as confessor to St. Theresa then as prior of the order. His reforming efforts did not go unnoticed by enemies of the reforms. In 1577 he was kidnapped by his rivals and imprisoned. Ironically, imprisonment spurred St. John to begin writing; first, *The Spiritual Canticles,* but later that same year producing not only *The Dark Night of the Soul,* but also its counterpart *Ascent of Mt. Carmel.* After his escape from imprisonment, and in the latter part of his life, he founded a number of convents and monasteries, taking a growing role in the leadership of his order. Having never fully recovered from his imprisonment, St. John of the Cross died December 14, 1591. In 1726, 135 years later, Benedict XIII officially canonized John of the Cross.

St. John's writings are marked by the singular and overwhelming influence of Scripture. As Robert Lechner observes, "Efforts to point out the influences upon the work of St. John of the Cross have been somewhat unsatisfactory. The direct influence of Scripture alone seems sure and clear" (Lechner, "St. John of the Cross and Sacramental Experience," pp. 544-551). Thus, St. John of the Cross draws repeatedly from Scripture's most tortured souls. "The Scriptural description of the interior sufferings of Jeremiah, Job, and the Psalmist became for him a divine blueprint of the suffering that all must undergo in some form or other if God's life is to hold full sway in their natural faculties" (Barnabas, "The Use of Scripture in the Spiritual Theology of St. John of the Cross," pp. 6-17).

St. John's writing is noted for a thorough, even romantic, sense of love from God to the individual believer. "If anything, his spirituality is closest to that of the 'Song of Songs' – ecstatic, erotic, sensual and loving – a poem he loved throughout his life and that influenced much of his own mature writing" ("St. John of the Cross"). From this remarkable connection of intimacy and suffering, we begin to understand how St. John might overshadow other historical figures as the go to liminal theologian. St. John of the Cross composed works which provide readers with an unparalleled depth concerning times of trial and struggle. Robert Lechner describes his writing as follows: "They are works of spiritual formation … where theology becomes mystery, morality becomes spirituality and liturgy becomes life" ("St. John of the Cross and Sacramental Experience," pp. 550).

In his work, St. John of the Cross makes it clear that the experiences of liminality and the dark night are universal among believers. As Gracia Fay (Bouwman) Ellwood describes St. John of the Cross's theology, "Sooner or later in the course of one's salvation God puts Himself into competition with things – all things, good and bad – and demands a choice involving complete surren-

der and total sacrifice" (Ellwood, "Conflicts of the dark night,"
pp. 16-18). St John of the Cross says, regarding new believers,
"For, as I have said, God now sees that they have grown a little,
and are becoming strong enough to lay aside their swaddling clothes
and be taken from the gentle breast; so He sets them down from
His arms and teaches them to walk on their own feet; which they
feel to be very strange" (*Ascent*, p. 414). The believer enters a paradoxical world of trial and suffering, a world God himself brings
them into, "When they are going about these spiritual exercises
with the greatest delight and pleasure, and when they believe that
the sun of Divine favor is shining most brightly upon them, God
turns all this light of theirs into darkness" (*Ascent*, p. 414).

As we have noted in every other example of liminality thus far
presented, the dark night of the soul is a time of painful self-dis-
covery and of reorienting priorities. St. John of the Cross himself
writes, "This is the first and principal benefit caused by this arid and
dark night of contemplation: the knowledge of oneself and of one's
misery" (*Ascent*, 425). The liminal experience of the soul prevents
any notion of rest for the person in the midst of it. "[God] allows
[the soul] not to find attraction or sweetness in anything whatso-
ever" (St. John of the Cross, 415). As per the paradoxical natural of
the dark night, the soul is brought into full contact with God within such an experience. "For in such a way does this dark night of
contemplation absorb and immerse the soul in itself, and so near
does it bring the soul to God, that it protects and delivers it from
all that is not God" (*Ascent*, 486).

The individual person in the dark night sees his own sinful
nature and thus believes he or she has been abandoned by God.
"But what the sorrowful soul feels most in this condition is its clear
perception, as it thinks, that God has abandoned it, and, in His
abhorrence of it, has flung it into darkness; it is a grave and piteous
grief for it to believe that God has forsaken it" (*Ascent*, p. 447).

Naturally this will cause the individual pain, as St. John writes,
"when the said Divine light assails the soul, it must needs cause
it to suffer" (*Ascent*, 462). Each individual experiences his or her
time of abandonment, and darkness on the basis of his or her own

needs and God's intentions for the particular person. St. John seems to indicate that the more God is at work in an individual the more the individual will feel the darkness within his soul. "The brighter and purer is supernatural and Divine light, the more it darkens the soul, and that, the less bright and pure is it, the less dark it is to the soul" (*Ascent*, pp. 455-456). St. John further indicates that God himself determines according to his own will the duration and experience of the dark night for each individual.

> For how long a time the soul will be held in this fasting and penance of sense, cannot be said with any certainty; for all do not experience it after one manner, neither do all encounter the same temptations. For this is meted out by the will of God, in conformity with the greater or the smaller degree of imperfection which each soul has to purge away. In conformity, likewise, with the degree of love of union to which God is pleased to raise it, he will humble it with greater or less intensity or in greater or less time. (*Ascent*, p. 435).

In the midst of the trials of the dark night certain character traits and qualities are enhanced or indeed grown from within the believer's experience. For example, "And the most proper form of this chastisement ... the soul is truly humiliated in preparation for the exaltation which it is to experience" (*Ascent*, 435).

Even though each experience of the liminality is unique, the outcome and benefits for individuals are surprisingly and uniformly similar. Rather than a progressive cause and effect of the liminal experience on the soul, the dark night causes a constellation of benefits and changes within the person and the relationship between God and his children. "Wherein the soul is purged and stripped according to the spirit, and subdued and made ready for the union of love with God " (*Ascent*, 413). This connection with God comes with a number of benefits: "And that in this night the soul obtains these four benefits which we have here described (namely, delight of peace, habitual remembrance and thought of God, cleanness and purity of soul and the practice of the virtues which we have just described)" (*Ascent*, p. 431).

The dark night of the soul provides a greater sense of God's peace. "By means of that war of the dark night, as has been said, the soul is combated and purged after two manners ... with all its faculties and desires, the soul attains to an enjoyment of peace and rest" (*Ascent*, p. 515). Peace is not simply restored but enhanced by the experience through the dark night of the soul. As Peter Tyler remarks, "The genius of John was that he recognized that we do not vanquish the appetites through our own efforts and the denial of them, but by surrendering to the 'higher and better love' of Jesus Christ" ("St. John of the Cross," pp. 301-310). Indeed, it is through the dark night that the soul is brought to an increased sense of God's love: "Thus, being exhausted, withered and thoroughly tried in the fire of this dark contemplation, and having driven away every kind of evil spirit ... it may have a simple and pure disposition ... so that it may feel the rare and sublime touches of Divine love" (St. John of the Cross, 459).

The rest and peace a believer grows into stand alongside an intimate relationship with God marked by a sanctified, holy soul. The soul is "purged and healthy, so that it may feel the rare and sublime touches of Divine love, wherein it will see itself divinely transformed" (*Ascent*, p. 459). As such there results also a spiritual wholeness: "Like one who has begun a cure.... By this means it becomes healed of many imperfections, and exercises itself in many virtues in order to make itself meet for the said love" (*Ascent*, 422-423).

Although St. John of the Cross named his meditation *The Dark Night of the Soul*, it is clear that his work is concerned more with the extent to which God's love moves in extraordinary ways to ensure the believer's sanctification. Neither is this work a clinical, cold sanctification, detached from intimacy or warmth. Rather, God works to ensure a relationship with his child, one that is of abiding trust. The individual is placed in difficult and trying circumstances in order that he or she may come to more clearly trust God is good and loving in all circumstances.

CHAPTER 7

JOHN NEWTON

"How could the power of grace be manifest, either to you, in you, or by you, without afflictions?" The above statement by John Newton is in a letter entitled *Difficulties of the Ministry*, and it may very well sum up John Newton's notions of suffering and affliction (Newton, *Selected Letters*). In many of his letters there exists a fundamental belief that suffering, though un-beckoned, is ultimately a positive force in the life of the believer.[1] In this section we will demonstrate how Newton's insights help to clarify our own picture of the Christian's experience of liminality.

John Newton is best known today as the author of the hymn "Amazing Grace." Newton was an only child whose parents were Congregationalists (Armstrong, *Patron Saints for Postmoderns*, p. 113). In his early years he was deeply influenced by his mother's faith. However, while serving as a sailor in his teens he temporarily abandoned it (*Patron Saints*, p. 114-115). John Newton eventually became a sea captain, including captaining ships involved in the African slave trade. Through contact with committed Christians along the way and the writings of Thomas à Kempis, Newton regained the faith he once had in his youth. By 1757 he was actively seeking ordination as a Church of England priest. Ordained in 1764, Newton went on to be a rector in several parishes throughout England. John Wesley describes Newton as "designed by divine providence for a healer of breaches, a reconciler of honest but prejudiced men, and an uniter" (*Patron Saints*, p. 113). In Newton's own day his fame and influence heralded from the correspondence he kept with a wide swath of the English population. The film entitled

---

1 Note that this is not an argument pertaining to or touching John Newton's theodicy. The selections in this paper merely pertain to the smaller issue of suffering and the life of the believer.

for his most famous hymn depicts in part his correspondence with William Wilberforce (Apted, *Amazing Grace*). It is not uncommon to find letters written to fellow clergy, noblemen, fellow sea captains, or even to an inquiring housewife (http://www.gracegems. org/Newton/additional_letters_of_newton.htm).

Three letters of Newton's stand out as particularly helpful toward the larger task at hand. The first letter is entitled, *Grace in the Blade*, the second letter, *Grace in the Ear*, and finally *The Full Corn in the Ear*. Their overall subject area is personal sanctification. As he states in the opening line of the first of these "Omicron Letters," "I sit down to give you my general views of a progressive work of grace, in the several stages of a believer's experience" (Newton, *The Works of John Newton*, p. 197). The letters themselves were penned by Newton as part of a larger collection of 41 letters intended for publication and were written to and in conversation with the Rev. Dr. Thomas Haweis.

Thomas Haweis was a younger contemporary of John Newton. As a young man his family apprenticed him to an apothecary and a physician. His family was at the time too poor to send him to university. However, in the course of events a local Vicar paid for Haweis's university education (Henwick, *The Free Church of England*, p. 21). In 1764 Haweis accepted a call to All Saints, Aldwincle Northhamptonshire. He served as rector at the church until his death in 1820. Haweis, like Newton, was noted for writing hymns and had close relationships with the leading evangelicals in his day (*Free Church*, 21). Thus, Haweis provides both an interesting contrast to the ministry path of Newton, but having a common foundation rooted in their evangelical leaning Anglicanism.

The three "Omicron Letters" trace the believer through a different stage of the Christian life and an attentive reader will clearly see how Newton in part is describing liminality. His dominant metaphor throughout the three letters is taken from Mark 4:28: "But when the grain is ripe, at once he puts in the sickle, because the harvest has come." Newton is fully aware that he is making a generalization but nevertheless feels justified in doing so for the sake of his overall argument.

The Lord leads all his people effectually and savingly to the knowledge of the same essential truths, but in such a variety of methods, that it will be needful, in this disquisition, to set aside, as much as possible, such things as may be only personal and occasional in the experience of each, and to collect those only which, in a greater or less degree, are common to them all. (Newton, *Works*, p. 197)

The first letter, "Grace in the Blade," discusses *A*, the unbeliever turned new believer. As with Augustine, there is a tug of war raging in a would-be believer's heart, between what he wishes to believe, and what he fears stands against him. For Newton, *A* may have a healthy awareness of God's law and his circumstance as sinner. "He believes the word of God, sees and feels things to be as they are described, hates and avoids sin, because he knows it is displeasing to God." (Newton, *Works*, p. 200). In the end, however, *A* has not arrived at a place of surrender. "He fears lest the compassionate Savior should spurn him from his feet" (*Works*, p. 200). *A*'s awareness of God is not meant to be a place of rest but rather, "to encourage him to press forward" (Newton, *Works*, p. 201). When *A* has indeed finally turned the corner on genuine faith in Christ, and having been granted by God's grace a measure of success, one reads in Newton's description a naivety of youthful spiritual energy. "His zeal is likewise lively; and may be, for want of more experience, too importunate and forward" (Newton, *Works*, p. 200). In the course of time, *A* eventually arrives at the second stage of a believer's sanctification.

The second letter describes *B*, the confirmed and growing believer. Rather than grasping at the eternal reality of a loving God, *B* is characterized by an assurance of Christ's sufficiency for all suitable needs and a peace in the knowledge that *B* is now firmly in Christ's "camp." Despite this newfound identity, *B*, in Newton's estimation, is paradoxically noted for conflict and deepening of the person's faith. In this stage of spiritual growth Newton believes one is most likely to come into conflict with the prince of darkness. "He is surrounded by invisible spiritual enemies, the extent of whose power and subtlety he is yet to learn by painful experience" (Newton, *Works*, p. 206). John Newton writes on a separate occasion and to a different correspondent: "There are particular seasons when temptations are suited to our frames, tempers, and situations; and there are times when [God] is pleased to withdraw, and to permit Satan's approach, that we may feel how vile we are in ourselves." A parallel, though not perfect, can be drawn to Christ's temptation. On the eve of the temptation Christ had publicly been declared "beloved son" only to be confronted and challenged by Satan on the grounds of his newly declared identity. Likewise, Newton's *B* is clearly a new man, but is immediately challenged by the enemy. The believer finds himself in a newfound conflict internally. "He knows that his heart is 'deceitful, and desperately wicked,' but he does not, he cannot, know, at first, the full meaning of that expression" (Newton, *Works*, p. 206).

Not only does Newton's assessment parallel Christ's temptation in the wilderness, one of the three great metaphors of liminality, but he directly describes the experience of *B* as a wilderness. For *B* "has a wilderness before him, of which he is not aware" (*Works*, p. 205). Liminality is characterized by the paradox of intimacy and struggle. Newton describes *B* in virtually the same way, using the life of King Hezekiah as an example. "I suppose he knew more of God, and of himself, in the time of his sickness, than he had ever done before" (Newton, *Works*, p. 207).

The fully formed believer, *C*, is described by Newton as characterized chiefly by contemplation. In the end of this stage it is the believer's demeanor and outlook on life that is most strikingly different from the earlier stages of growth. Newton asserts that the life of the mature believer is not free from struggle; it is the manner in which he deals with struggle that makes him distinct from his maturing self. Newton describes the believer as one who has, "learned, with the Apostle, not only to suffer want, but, (which is perhaps the harder lesson) how to abound. A palace would be a prison to him, without the Lord's presence; and with this a prison would be a palace" (Newton, *Works*, p. 214). A few lines later Newton states, "Therefore he [*C*] is not afraid of evil tidings; but when the hearts of others shake like the leaves of a tree, he is fixed, trusting in the

Lord, who he believes can and will make good every loss, sweeten every bitter, and appoint all things to work together for his advantage" (Newton, *Works*, p. 214). In the end, to the mature believer, Christ and his glory are the ultimate concern.

> But C has attained to more enlarged views: he has a desire to depart and to be with Christ, which would be importunate if he considered only himself; but his chief desire is, that God may be glorified in him, whether by his life or by his death. He is not his own; nor does he desire to be his own; but, so that the power of Jesus may be manifested in him, he will take pleasure in infirmities, in distresses, in temptations; and, though he longs for heaven, he would be content to live as long as Methuselah upon earth, if, by thing he could do or suffer, the will and glory of God might be promoted. (Newton, *Works*, p. 217)

Newton is firmly convinced of God's role in the believer's growth into maturity. He writes, "You owe your growth in these respects in a great measure to His blessing upon those afflictions which He has prepared for you, and sanctified to you" (Newton, *Selected Letters and Poems of John Newton*, loc. 2005). Indeed, Newton argues in another letter that God uses struggle and suffering as a catalyst for maturity.

> So, in a long course of ease, the powers of the new man would certainly languish; the soul would grow soft, indolent, cowardly, and faint; and therefore the Lord appoints His children such dispensations as make them strive and struggle, and pant; they must press through a crowd, swim against a stream, endure hardships, run, wrestle, and fight; and thus their strength grows in the using. By these things, likewise, they are made more willing to leave the present world, to which we are prone to cleave too closely in our hearts when our path is very smooth. (*Selected Letters*, loc. 1991).

Why does God allow the believer to face these various struggles and griefs? The believer endures such things in order for God's glory to be manifested. Writing in the second of the "Omicron letters"

Newton states, "[God] would not suffer sin to remain in them, if he did not purpose to over-rule it, for the fuller manifestation of the glory of his grace and wisdom, and for the making his salvation more precious to their souls" (*Selected Letters*, loc. 932-933).

Newton sees this suffering, often times individualized for the believer's sake, as a necessary crucible for godly character.

> Again, how could we, without sufferings, manifest the nature and truth of Gospel-grace! What place should we then have for patience, submission, meekness, forbearance, and a readiness to forgive, if we had nothing to try us, either from the hand of the Lord, or from the hand of men! A Christian without trials would be like a mill without wind or water; the contrivance and design of the wheel-work within would be unnoticed and unknown, without something to put it in motion from without. (*Selected Letters*, loc. 1985).

In one of Newton's letters addressed to Mrs. H – entitled "The School of Suffering," he tells her, " I suppose you are still in the school of the cross, learning the happy art of extracting real good out of seeming evil, and to grow tall by stooping" (*Selected Letters*, loc. 1972). In a letter entitled "Trusting God and Honouring his Methods," Newton tells the anonymous recipient, "All your pains and trials, all that befalls you in your own person, or that affects you upon the account of others, shall in the end prove to your advantage. And your peace does not depend upon any change of circumstance which may appear desirable, but in having your will bowed to the Lord's will, and made willing to submit all to His disposal and management" (*Selected Letters*, loc. 305). In the final "Omicron Letter" Newton states that the mature believer "[has a view] of his own vileness, unworthiness, and ignorance, and of the Divine sovereignty, wisdom, and love teach him to be content in every state" (*Selected Letters*, loc. 1013).

If there is a dominant secondary image in Newton's description of the believer's sanctification, it is a comparison with the experiences of the Israelites in Exodus. In the letter entitled, "The School of Suffering," Newton makes this comparison explicit.

Had Israel enjoyed their former peace and prosperity in Egypt, when Moses came to invite them to Canaan, I think they would hardly have listened to him. But the Lord suffered them to be brought into great trouble and bondage, and then the news of deliverance was more welcome, yet still they were but half willing, and they carried a love [of] the flesh-pots of Egypt with them into the wilderness. We are like them: though we say this world is vain and sinful, we are too fond of it; and though we hope for true happiness only in Heaven, we are often well content to stay longer here. But the Lord sends afflictions one after another to quicken our desires, and to convince us that this cannot be our rest. (*Selected Letters*, loc. 1995-1999).

For the person transitioning from *A* to *B* Newton says the following:

[A] like Israel, has been delivered from Egypt by great power and a stretched-out arm, has been pursued and terrified by many enemies, has given himself up for lost again and again. He has at last seen his enemies destroyed, and has sung the song of Moses and the Lamb upon the banks of the Red Sea. Then he commences B. Perhaps, like Israel, he thinks his difficulties are at an end, and expects to go on rejoicing till he enters the promised land. But, alas! his difficulties are in a manner but beginning; he has a wilderness before him, of which he is not aware. (*Works*, p. 205)

At the end of the Christian journey the Christian can look back and memorialize the events of his or her life. And once again it is the experiences and images of the Israelites that Newton uses to make his comparison: "It is a part of C's daily employment to look back upon the way by which the Lord has led him; and while he reviews the Ebenezers he has set up all along the road, he sees, in almost an equal number, the monuments of his own perverse returns, and how he has in a thousand instances rendered to the Lord evil for good" (*Works*, p. 212).

In summary, one can define three contributions of John Newton's theology toward understanding liminality. First, Newton both echoes what has previously been discussed in connection with liminality, as well as adding to our understanding of the place of liminality. Nowhere else do we see more clearly how liminality is a part of the everyday experience of the Christian believer. Newton acknowledges, as Augustine does, that liminality is and can be a part of the conversion process. Second, God is orchestrating events which bring believers into times of trial and testing. Third, the employment of wilderness and Israel's experience are examples of these dry seasons and the paradox of their intimacy with God as a result. Newton adds to our understanding of liminal time with the emphasis on the ubiquitous nature of these times in the life of a Christian. For Newton liminal time is necessary part of sanctification.

In the end, it would be wise to listen to Newton's own advice on this subject of liminal space. He writes the following in his letter "Honoring God and Trusting His Methods":

> Be not surprised to find yourself poor, helpless, and vile; all whom He favors and teaches will find themselves so. The more grace increases, the more we shall see to abase us in our own eyes; and this will make the Savior and His salvation more precious to us. He takes His own wise methods to humble you, and to prove you, and I am sure He will do you good in the end. (*Selected Letters*, loc. 308).

CHAPTER 7

HENRI NOUWEN

Henri Nouwen was a keen observer of the brokenness of the human heart. Nouwen, though rarely discussing liminality by name, expresses in his writings many of the hallmarks explored in this volume. In many of his books, particularly *The Wounded Healer* and *Spiritual Formation,* he describes a process entered into by the leading of a loving God. These times are often paradoxical and confusing, where a person may feel alone and isolated even while experiencing a renewed sense of God's presence and love. Finally, Nouwen informs his readers that times of inner wrestling spur growth and maturity in a leader, igniting new ministry, and as a result a healthier Christian community.

According to Michael Higgins and Kevin Burns, Nouwen wrote more than 50 books along with numerous articles and introductions (Higgins, *Genius Born of Anguish*, 150). Many of these books centered on the spiritual life of the believer and the believer's place in community. Nouwen may be best known as the author of two slim volumes, *The Return of the Prodigal Son* and *The Wounded Healer.* His ability to speak of the heart's mysteries arose not only from years of writing and working as a psychologist and pastor, but also from his very own struggles. Throughout his many volumes he provides an articulated understanding of where and how the liminal process takes place, and also how this process advances the health of the community and the leadership ability of the individual engaged in the liminal experience. As Nouwen states, "The great illusion of leadership is to think that man can be led out of the desert by someone who has never been there" (Nouwen, *Spiritual Formation*, p. 42).

By all outward appearances Henri Nouwen had a fulfilling life of service and achievement. He was born in 1932 in the Netherlands, and was ordained to the Roman Catholic priesthood 25

years later in 1957. He received doctorates in both psychology and
theology and went on to teach in both fields. His professorships
included postings at Yale Divinity School and Harvard Divinity
School. However, it seemed the outward success did little to mask
his inward wrestlings: "Those who knew him were aware of how
deep his wounds ran. He was afflicted by an inordinate need for
affection and affirmation; he was beset by anxieties about his identity and self-worth; there seemed to be a void within that could
not be filled" (Ellsberg, "Thomas Merton, Henri Nouwen, and the
Living Gospel," pp. 346).

Nouwen left the academic world and became the priest in
residence at L'Arche Daybreak community in 1986. Daybreak was
part of a larger series of communities worldwide that served individuals with profound mental and physical disabilities.

> Nouwen was assigned to care for one of the handicapped
> residents – in fact, one of the most severely handicapped adults
> in the community, a young man named Adam, who could not
> talk or move by himself.... But to his surprise he found this an
> occasion for deep inner conversion. Adam was not impressed
> by Nouwen's books or his fame or his genius as a public speak-
> er. But through this mute and helpless man, Nouwen began to
> know what it meant to be "beloved" of God. ("Living Gospel,"
> pp. 340-354).

It was not an easy or painless transition for Nouwen. Shortly
after his first year at Daybreak, Nouwen went through his own, incredibly dark experience. "After his first year at Daybreak Nouwen
suffered a nervous breakdown – the culmination of long suppressed
tensions. For months he could barely talk or leave his room. Now
he was the helpless one, mutely crying out for some affirmation of
his existence." In the end, however, Nouwen would report to his
friends and colleagues, "I now know that while I felt completely
abandoned, God didn't leave me alone" ("Living Gospel," pp. 340-
354).

Much like Julian of Norwich, Nouwen's writing is an interior
driven landscape. His writing focuses on the inner struggle of the

Christian, and how this struggle and wrestling bring growth and maturity. Nouwen writes in *The Return of the Prodigal Son,* "Every time I touch that dreadful yet fruitful emptiness in myself, I know that I can welcome anyone there without condemnations and offer hope.... In that emptiness, God's unconditional love could be sensed" (Nouwen, *The Return of the Prodigal Son,* pp. 132-133). Much of Nouwen's work consists of paradox and the duel reality that what is difficult is also what is blessed. As previously discussed in this book, this dual reality is one of the chief characteristics of liminality in the life of a believer. "I was experiencing my deepest sadness – right in the middle of all that, something new was happening. Right there in the pain, I began to get in touch with a joy that was deeper and more profound. In human brokenness new life is born. In the tears and grief, joy and happiness are found" (*Spiritual Formation,* p. 42).

Nouwen acknowledges difficult times are often periods which one is led into by the sovereign will of God. He writes, "When we let love speak within us, we are led into places where we often would rather not go" (Nouwen, *Letters to Marc about Jesus,* p. 76). Such periods are often repeated in the life of a believer. In an article appearing in the journal *Sojourners,* Nouwen describes what he terms "displacement" as a spiritual discipline, a description that could just as easily be entitled liminality. "Displacement is the discipline necessary to prevent us from being caught in the net of the ordinary and proper. In order for displacement to be a real discipline, however, it must be a voluntary displacement, a displacement which we can affirm from within when we have little or no control over the external circumstances" (Nouwen, "Voluntary Displacement," p. 15). As Nouwen refers to it, this place is hidden from the view of outsiders, allowing God to work in the secret places of the human heart. Nouwen wrote in his book *Letters to Marc,* "Whereas the way of the world is to insist on publicity, celebrity, popularity, and getting maximum exposure, God prefers to work in secret.... In God's sight, the things that really matter seldom take place in public" (*Letters to Marc,* p. 68). A few pages later Nouwen continues, "The mystery of the spiritual life is that Jesus desires to meet us in the seclusion of our own heart, to make his love known to us there, to free us from our fears, and to make our own deepest self known to us. In the privacy of our heart, therefore, we can learn not only to know Jesus, but through Jesus to know ourselves as well" (*Letters to Marc*, p. 74). Along with this hidden work is the willingness of the one being drawn into the liminal experience to obediently follow God into such times.

> Trust and gratitude are the disciplines for the conversion of the elder son. And I have come to know them through my own experience. Without trust, I cannot let myself be found. Trust is that deep inner conviction that the Father wants me home. As long as I doubt that I am worth finding and put myself down as less loved than my younger brothers and sisters, I cannot be found. (*Prodigal*, p. 84)

Just because we walk into these periods of God's working and testing does not mean that the pain associated with the Christian life is removed: "To grieve is to experience the pain of your life and face the dark abyss where nothing is clear or settled, where everything is shifting and changing" (*Spiritual Formation* p. 42). For Nouwen, growth takes place in the struggle of the human condition. Nouwen writes succinctly, "The Christian way of life does not take away our loneliness" (Nouwen, *The Wounded Healer*, p. 86). Pain, Nouwen states, is necessary, indeed indispensable, to finding wholeness. "You can never get to this joy if you dare not cry, if you do not have the courage to weep, if you don't take the opportunity to experience pain" (*Spiritual Formation*, p. 42). Nouwen compares the process of the Christian life to that of a stonemason or sculptor chipping away at his carving to reveal the image underneath. (*Spiritual Formation*, p. 66).

What then is the purpose of God's leading the individual into periods of liminality with no guarantee of relief from pain and hurt? There are at least two reasons for such experiences. The first is the formation of a qualified leader and teacher. Ministry begins and is authentic only as one is willing to enter into these periods and serve others by being an example to others. Reflecting on Mark 1:32-39, Nouwen states, "It is in the lonely place, where Jesus enters into intimacy with the Father, that his ministry is born" (*Spiritual Formation*, p. 21). In *The Wounded Healer*, his most deliberate articulation of what it means to be priest, Nouwen writes, "The Christian leader is, therefore, first of all, a man who is willing to put his own articulated faith at the disposal of those who ask his help. In this sense he is a servant of servants, because he is the first to enter the promised but dangerous land, the first to tell those who are afraid what he has seen, heard and touched" (Wounded Healer, p. 39). Being a priest or minister of the gospel goes beyond filling one's bag of tricks to an incarnational expression of love. "In the context [of] pastoral conversation it is not merely a skillful use of conversational techniques to manipulate people into the Kingdom of God, but a deep human encounter in which a man is willing to put his own faith and doubt, his own hope and despair, his own light and darkness at the disposal of others who want to find a way through their confusion and touch the solid core of faith" (*Wounded Healer*, p. 39).

The second reason for experiencing such struggle is in fact for the sake of the community. When the leader has learned and continues to abide in the process of being sanctified in difficult circumstances, a healthy open community can be nurtured in the wake. "A Christian community is therefore a healing community not because wounds are cured and pains are alleviated, but because openings are occasions for a new vision. Mutual confession then becomes a mutual deepening of hope, and sharing weakness becomes a reminder to one and all of the coming strength" (*Wounded Healer*, p. 94). In a community where people have the freedom to be themselves, life is found. "No man can stay alive when nobody is waiting for him" (*Wounded Healer*, p. 66).

As has been articulated above, Nouwen consistently returns to themes of displacement, wilderness and inner wrestling in his writing. In numerous ways and in various writings he is outlining a theology of liminality without using that term specifically. However, the hallmarks of liminality are present: the negative feelings of inner psychological tension; the growth through pain; the confusing emotions of sensing both God's absence and presence in the midst of this time; and the positive positioning for a new ministry and healthier leadership in the future.

CHAPTER 8

CONCLUSION-LIMINALITY AND THE BELIEVER

In attempting to understand liminality it is prudent to restate our given definition: "This bewildering phenomena, familiar in the Jewish and Christian Scriptures, [creating] for a time either contextual or inner dissonance which, when its work is complete, is often understood by the person involved as having facilitated considerable personal growth and change" (Franks). From this we can define liminality with five further characteristics. First, liminality is part of the interior journey of the Christian. The exception to this of course is when liminality is entered into by an entire community such as the Israelites after the exodus or during the exile. Second, the context for the individual and this inner journey is that of community, the church. Third, pain and prayer are the instruments that God chooses to use during liminality to affect his desired outcome within the believer. Fourth, the purpose of liminality in the life of the believer is primarily to teach obedience. But as St. John of the Cross demonstrates, this is an obedience born out of intimate joy and belonging. And thus, lastly, in obedience to God, one is properly prepared for ministry and service. The believer is sanctified by the Holy Spirit and able to enjoy a fuller and richer expression of personal holiness and relationship with others.

Liminality is an interior spiritual reality where one enters the interior castle of one's soul to battle himself. As Augustine described his own experience, "I went into myself ... lash[ed] my soul" (*Confessions*, 194). Four of the five historical figures examined here emphasize that liminal reality is experienced squarely in the heart and mind of the believer. One exception in the historical survey is John Newton. Newton, however, is taking the wide angle view of liminality. He examines the scope of the believer's entire life.

Added to the evidence from our historical figures are the numerous times we find the Psalms to be fertile ground for describing liminality. The Psalms are poetry and song expressing the feelings of the individual worshiper. Christ's experience of liminality is the natural exception to this rule. However, without a sin nature, Christ's experience of liminality, which comes in the desert temptations, must by default originate from outside this inner personal context.

As much as liminality takes place within the human heart it is not without its proper context in the community of the church. Nouwen said that one member of his community "encouraged me to struggle through whatever needed to be suffered to reach true inner freedom" (*Prodigal*, p. 21). Nouwen and Newton both engage in pastoral dialogue via letters to assist and direct fellow believers through liminal experiences. In the exodus and the wilderness, Israel is, among other things, defining community for themselves, and the experiences become definitive for the entire community. Likewise, in the exile, there is a back and forth between Jeremiah and the captives in Babylon. Jeremiah urges his fellow Israelites to remain in the difficult tension of exile, encouraging them to stay the course.

The tools in which God affects his purpose in liminal experiences are prayer and pain. One might suggest that prayer and pain are the means by which God affects the change he is seeking in the believer. Walter Brueggemann, speaking of the exile, notes how integral pain is to determining an individual's future. "If we do not experience the pain, rage, and disease that goes with such disequilibrium, we may be missing out on our call" (*Hopeful Imagination*, p. 23). Christ's liminal experience began with a 40-day fast that left him weak and tempted by his hunger. Julian in her writing states clearly that pain is often a tool for God's use in the process of sanctification: "God willeth that we know that He keepeth us even alike secure in woe and in weal. And for profit of man's soul, a man is sometime *left to himself*, although sin is not always the cause" (*Revelations of Divine Love*, p. 441). Newton echoes Julian's sentiment. "All your pains and trials, all that befalls you in your own person, or that affects you upon the account of others, shall in the end prove to your advantage" (*Selected Letters*, loc. 305).

As regards to prayer, each of the Psalms discussed in this book have been first person prayers to God. They plead for God's response in the midst of difficult circumstances. Likewise, Julian of Norwich's and Augustine's manuscripts are taken as a formal prayer and meditation in prayer. It is not a stretch to see prayer as a constant backdrop in which the whole of the narratives are taking place within each of the metaphors and authors discussed.

Liminality effectively creates obedient people. Jesus's temptation in the wilderness was a test of his obedience to God's will. R.T. France and Craig Blomberg, in their interpretations of Matthew's account of the temptation, point toward Christ's obedience in contrast with human disobedience. Jonah learns the lengths to which God will work in order that he may obediently do the will of Yahweh and preach to Nineveh. Newton describes the result of the believer's growth as one in which he is faithful in all circumstances.

However, this obedience is not an end into itself. Obedience leads to ministry and calling as well as intimacy. In every instance cited in this book, within liminality, obedience leads to ministry and calling. The Israelites' wandering in the wilderness leads to taking the Promised Land and becoming a people set apart for Yahweh. The exiles recommit themselves to this commission, and unlike their exodus forefathers, live idol-free. Through the tomb Christ initiates a new faith community which bears his name and proclaims the good news of his death and resurrection. For Augustine, liminality results in his ministry to and in the church. Julian of Norwich sees a deepened calling to obedience and identification with her savior. Newton and Nouwen make great effort to highlight how liminal obedience leads to faithful witness and ministry. As Nouwen says so succinctly, "The great illusion of leadership is to think that man can be led out of the desert by someone who has never been there" (*Spiritual Formation*, p. 42).

The artist and cultural critic Makato Fujimura takes this one tantalizing step further. In his book *Culture Care* he presents an old English word which roughly translates into "border stalker."

In a chapter entitled "Leadership from the Margins," Makato describes a figure that is between countries, living between nations and contexts (Makato, *Culture Core*, p. 39). Makato suggests a border stalker, one who lives in these liminal spaces, is also in a prime place to lead and speak into the lives of those planted within more well-established contexts. Thus, Makato seems to echo Peter's description of Christian life as both exilic and a place of leadership.

Obedience and leadership should not therefore be seen as drudgery, but as intimacy. As St. John of the Cross so boldly reminds the believer in his writing, "And thus, since the function of these virtues is the withdrawal of the soul from all that is less than God, their function is consequently that of joining it with God" (*Ascent*, p. 503).

In conclusion, since much of this book revolves around the nuancing of metaphors, allow one more metaphor to describe the larger picture of liminality – the blacksmith's smithy. We first should consider the Christian as the raw untempered steel of God's smithy. The changes wrought in the fire of the furnace are interior changes; the alignment of carbon atoms within the structure of the steel hardens and strengthens the blade. The smithy's shop, the tools of the blacksmith's trade (hammer, knives, water pail) are analogous to the church with its various purposes and proper uses. Prayer and pain are the necessary elements of heat and air that make the process effective. The tempest that is the heat and air make the steel take the form of the blacksmith's desire. The steel is literally bent to the will of the blacksmith's mind. The steel, obedient to the blacksmith's work, is then set free to be the sword, hammer, plough or anchor the blacksmith envisioned. Thus, in the hands of such a master craftsman, it rises above utilitarian use to something more akin to a fine work of art, cherished as much for its beauty as its utility. No one looks at a master blacksmith and wonders what he has made: the tool became artwork in the master's hand, and speaks to his skill and care. And as such, liminal experience speaks to the skills of an almighty God to lovingly craft his followers into instruments of his design.

BIBLIOGRAPHY

Anderson, A. A. *The Book of Psalms*. New Century Bible Commentary. Greenwood, SC: Attic Press, 1972.

Apted, Michael. *Amazing Grace*. Fox Searchlight, 2007.

Armstrong, Chris R. *Patron Saints for Postmoderns: 10 from the Past Who Speak to Our Future*. Downers Grove, IL: IVP Books, 2009.

Augustine. *The Confessions of Saint Augustine*. trans. John K. Ryan; New York, NY: Image Books Double Day,1960.

Barnabas, Mary Ahern. "The Use of Scripture in the Spiritual Theology of St. John of the Cross," *The Catholic Biblical Quarterly* 14, (January 1952): 6-17.

Baker, Denise Nowakowski. *Julian of Norwich's Showings: From Vision to Book*. Princeton, NJ: Princeton University Press, 1997.

Bakon, Shimon. "Exile and Return," *Jewish Bible Quarterly* 31, no. 2 (April 1, 2003): 101–108.

Beckwith, Carl L. ed. *Ezekiel, Daniel*. Reformation Commentary on Scripture. Old Testament 12. Downers Grove, IL: IVP Academic, 2012.

Blackburn, W. Ross. *The God Who Makes Himself Known: The Missionary Heart of the Book of Exodus*. New Studies in Biblical Theology 28. Downers Grove, IL: Apollos, 2012.

Blomberg, Craig. *Matthew*. The New American Commentary 22. Nashville: Broadman & Holman Publishers, 1992.

Boice, James Montgomery. *Psalms*. Grand Rapids, Mich: Baker Books, 1994.

Bratcher, Robert G., and William David Reyburn, *A Translator's Handbook on the Book of Psalms*. UBS Handbook Series. New York: United Bible Societies, 1991.

Brown, Brené, *Rising Strong*. New York: Spiegel & Grau, 2015.

Brown, Colin, and David Townsley, eds. *The New International Dictionary of New Testament Theology, Vol 3*. Grand Rapids, MI: Zondervan, 1975.

Brown, Peter Robert Lamont. *Augustine of Hippo: A Biography*. Berkeley: University of California Press, 2000.

Brueggemann, Walter. *Hopeful Imagination: Prophetic Voices in Exile*. Philadelphia: Fortress Press, 1986.

_____. *Cadences of Home: Preaching Among Exiles*. 1st ed. Louisville, Ky: Westminster John Knox Press, 1997.

Childs, Brevard S. *Biblical Theology of the Old and New Testaments: Theological Reflection on the Christian Bible*. Minneapolis: Fortress Press, 1993.

Edgerton, W. Dow. "Worship and transformation." *Chicago Theological Seminary Register* 75, no. 3 (September 1, 1985): 11-19. *ATLA Religion Database with ATLASerials*, EBSCOhost (accessed November 20, 2013).

Eldridge, Victor J. „Jeremiah, Prophet of Judgment," *Review & Expositor* 78, no. 3 (June 1, 1981): 319–330.

Eliot, T.S. *Complete Poems and Plays:1909-1965*. New York: Harcourt, Brace,1952.

Elliott, John Hall. *1 Peter: A New Translation with Introduction and Commentary*. The Anchor Bible v. 37B. New York: Doubleday, 2000.

Ellsberg, Robert. "Thomas Merton, Henri Nouwen, And The Living Gospel." *Merton Annual* 19 (2006): 340-354. Religion and Philosophy Collection. Web. 17 Aug. 2013.

Ellwood, Gracia Fay. "Conflicts of the dark night." *Reformed Journal* 11, no. 7 (July 1961): 16-18.

France, R.T. *The Gospel According to Matthew: An Introduction and Commentary,* (Eerdmans ed. Tyndale New Testament Commentaries, Leicester, England:; Grand Rapids, Mich: Inter-Varsity Press)1987.

_____. *The Gospel of Mark: A Commentary on the Greek Text.* New International Greek Testament Commentary. Grand Rapids, MI: Carlisle: W.B. Eerdmans; Paternoster Press, 2002.

Franks, Anne, and John Meteyard. "Liminality: The Transforming Grace of in-Between Places." *Journal Of Pastoral Care & Counseling* 61.3 (2007): 215-222.

Fujimura, Makoto. *Culture Care*, Fujimura Institute and International Arts Movement, 2014.

Goldingay, John. *Psalms*, Baker Commentary on the Old Testament Wisdom and Psalms, 3 volumes. (Ada, MI: Baker Academic, 2007).

Green, Joel B. *1 Peter*. The Two Horizons New Testament Commentary. Grand Rapids, MI; Cambridge, UK: William B. Eerdmans Publishing Company, 2007.

Grogan, Geoffrey. *Psalms. Two Horizons Old Testament Commentary,* Grand Rapids, MI: William B. Eerdmans Pub. Co, 2008.

Gruber, Judith. "Rethinking God in the interspace: interculturality as a locus theologicus." *Svensk Missionstidskrift* 100, no. 3 (January 1, 2012): 247-261.

Henwick, John. *The Free Church of England: Introduction to an Anglican Tradition.* 1st edition. London ; New York: Bloomsbury T&T Clark, 2004.

Higgins, Michael W. *Genius Born of Anguish: The Life & Legacy of Henri Nouwen.* New York : Toronto, Canada: Paulist Press ; Novalis, 2012.

Illman, Karl Johan. *"Psalm 88: a Lamentation without Answer,» (Scandinavian Journal Of The Old Testament* no. 1, 1991): 112-120.

Jenson, Phillip Peter. *Obadiah, Jonah, Micah: A Theological Commentary,* Library of Hebrew Bible/Old Testament Studies 496. New York: T & T Clark, 2008.

Jobes, Karen H. *1 Peter.* Baker Exegetical Commentary on the New Testament. Grand Rapids, MI: Baker Academic, 2005.

Jones, Barry. "Speaking to the Exiles." *Review & Expositor* 101 (2004): 177–200.

Jones, Douglas Rawlinson. *Jeremiah: Based on the Revised Standard Version.* New Century Bible Commentary. London : Grand Rapids: Marshall Pickering ; Eerdmans, 1992.

Kitchen, K. A. "midbar" *New Bible Dictionary,* edited by D. R. W. Wood and I. Howard Marshall, (Leicester, England; Downers Grove, IL: InterVarsity Press, 1996).

Kittel, Gerhard, Geoffrey W. Bromiley, and Gerhard Friedrich, eds., *Theological Dictionary of the New Testament.* Grand Rapids, MI: Eerdmans, 1964.

Lange, John Peter, Philip Schaff, Paul Kleinert, and Charles Elliott. *A Commentary on the Holy Scriptures: Jonah.* Bellingham, WA: Logos Bible Software, 2008.

Leal, R. B. *Wilderness In The Bible: Toward A Theology Of Wilderness.* New York; Bern: Lang, 2004.

Lechner, Robert F. "St. John of the Cross and Sacramental Experience," *Worship* 34.9 (1960): 544-551.

Lesquivit, Colomban and Andre-Alphonse Viard. "Exile." Pages 152-154 in *Dictionary Of Biblical Theology.* 2d ed. rev. and enl. edited by Xavier Léon-Dufour New York: Seabury Press, 1973.

Lewis, C. S. *Till We Have Faces.* Boston; Houghton Mifflin Harcourt. 1980. Kindle Edition.

Limburg, James. *Psalms.* Westminster Bible Companion. Louisville, KY: Westminster John Knox Press, 2000.

Louth, Andrew. *The Wilderness of God.* London: Darton, Longman and Todd, 1991.

Louw, Johannes P., and Eugene Albert Nida. *Greek-English Lexicon of the New Testament: Based on Semantic Domains, Vol. 1.* New York: United Bible Societies, 1996.

Marshall, I. Howard. *1 Peter.* The IVP New Testament Commentary Series, Downers Grove, IL: InterVarsity Press, 1991.

_____. *The Gospel of Luke: A Commentary on the Greek Text.* New International Greek Testament Commentary. Exeter: Paternoster Press, 1978.

Martin, T. W. *Metaphor and Composition in 1 Peter.* SBL Dissertation Series 131. Atlanta: Scholars Press, 1992.

Mein, Andrew. *Ezekiel and the Ethics of Exile.* Oxford Theological Monographs. Oxford; New York: Oxford University Press, 2001.

Miller, Gordon L. *The Way of the English Mystics: An Anthology and Guide for Pilgrims.* Ridgefield, Conn: Morehouse Pub, 1996.

Julian of Norwich, *Revelations of Divine Love*. Waxkeep Publishing. Kindle Edition, Oct 23, 2013.

Newton, John "Additional Letters of John Newto." Grace Gems, 2016. http://www.gracegems.org/Newton/additional_letters_of_newton.htm. Accessed 26 January 2014.

Newton, John (2010-03-29). *Selected Letters and Poems of John Newton*. Puritansermons.com. Kindle Edition.

Newton, John. *The Works of John Newton*. Edinburgh ; Carlisle, Pa: Banner of Truth Trust, 1985.

Nolland John. *The Gospel of Matthew: A Commentary on the Greek Text*. New International Greek Testament Commentary. Grand Rapids, MI; Carlisle: W.B. Eerdmans; Paternoster Press, 2005.

Nouwen, Henri J. M. *Letters to Marc about Jesus*. San Francisco: HarperOne, 1988.

Nouwen, Henri J M., Rebecca Laird, and Michael Christensen. *Spiritual Formation: Following The Movements of the Spirit*. San Francisco: HarperCollins, 2010.

Nouwen, Henri J. M. *The Return of the Prodigal Son: A Story of Homecoming*. New York: Image, 1993.

Nouwen, Henri J M. "Voluntary Displacement," *Sojourners* 6. (1977): 15. ATLA Religion Database with ATLASerials. Web. Accessed 13 Aug. 2013.

Nouwen, Henri J. M. *The Wounded Healer*. New York: Doubleday, 1979.

O'Donnell, James J. *Augustine Confessions: Volume 3: Commentary, Books 8-13*. Oxford: Oxford University Press, 2013.

Ortberg, John C., Jr, Marshall Shelley, and Eric Reed. "Holy Tension: Creating and Seizing Opportunities for Spiritual

Transformation: The Leadership Interview with John Ortberg." *Leadership* 25, no. 1 (December 1, 2004): 22-27.

Pain, Susanna. "What Does the Wilderness Look Like?" *Expository Times* 123.4 (2012): 183-185.

Patton, John. "Pastoral Ministry in a Fractured World," *Journal of Pastoral Care* 42, no. 1 (March 1, 1988): 26–36.

Parry, Robin. *Lamentations*. Two Horizons Old Testament Commentary. Grand Rapids, MI: Eerdmans, 2010.

Perrin, David B. "The Unique Contribution of John of the Cross to the Western Mystical Tradition." *Science et Esprit* 51, no. 2 (May 1999): 199–230.

Peterson, Eugene H. *The Message: The Bible in Contemporary Language*. Colorado Springs, CO: NavPress, 2005.

Rambo, Shelly and Catherine Keller. *Spirit and Trauma: A Theology of Remaining*. Louisville, KY: Westminster John Knox Press, 2010.

Rohr, Richard. *Everything Belongs: The Gift of Contemplative Prayer*. New York: Crossroads Books, 2003.

_____. *Near Occasions of Grace*. Maryknoll NY: Orbis Books. 1993.

Rowell, Geoffrey, Kenneth Stevenson, and Rowan Williams, eds. *Love's Redeeming Work: The Anglican Quest For Holiness*. Oxford: Oxford University Press, 2001.

Ryan, Robin. *God and the Mystery of Human Suffering: A Theological Conversation across the Ages*. New York: Paulist Press, 2011.

Ryken, Leland, James C. Wilhoit and Tremper Longman III eds. *Dictionary of Biblical Imagery*. Downers Grove, IL: IVP, 1998.

Schreiner, Thomas. *1, 2 Peter, Jude.* The New American Commentary, Vol. 37. Nashville: Broadman & Holman Publishers, 2003.

Smith, Billy K. and Franklin S. Page. *Amos, Obadiah, Jonah.* The New American Commentary, Vol. 19B. Nashville: Broadman & Holman Publishers, 1995.

Smith-Christopher, Daniel. *A Biblical Theology of Exile.* Minneapolis: Fortress Press, 2002.

Spurgeon, Charles H. *Morning and Evening: Daily Readings.* Complete and unabridged; New modern edition. Peabody, MA: Hendrickson Publishers, 2006.

Stuart, Douglas K. *Exodus.* The New American Commentary 2. Nashville: Holman Reference, 2006.

Steussy, Marti J. "On Being Broken." *Encounter* 72, no. 1 (March 1, 2011): 31–39.

St. John of the Cross, *Ascent of Mount Carmel, Dark Night of the Soul, & A Spiritual Canticle of the Soul and Bridegroom Christ.* Dublin, Ireland: Veritatis Splendor Publications, 2012.

Taylor, Barbara Brown. "Four Stops in the Wilderness." *Journal for Preachers* 24, no. 2 (January 1, 2001): 3–9.

Terrien, Samuel L. *The Psalms: Strophic Structure and Theological Commentary.* Eerdmans Critical Commentary. Grand Rapids, MI: William B. Eerdmans Pub, 2003.

Tiffany, Frederick C. Tiffany. "Facing the Wilderness/Encountering Chaos," *Quarterly Review* 18, no. 1 (March 1, 1998): 55–69.
Tuchman, Barbara Wertheim. *A Distant Mirror: The Calamitous 14th Century.* 1st trade ed. New York: Knopf, 1978.

Tyler, Peter. "St John of the Cross." *Journey to the Heart: Christian Contemplation through the Centuries.* Maryknoll, NY: Orbis Books, 2012.

Vassiliadis, Nikolaos P. *The Mystery of Death.* Athens: The Orthodox Brotherhood of Theologians, 1993.

Von Balthasar, Hans Urs. *Mysterium Paschale.* Translated by Aidan Nichols, San Fransico: Ignatius Press, 2012.

Watson, Duane Frederick. *First and Second Peter.* Paideia: Commentaries on the New Testament. Grand Rapids: Baker Academic, 2012.

Waltner, James H. *Psalms.* Believers Church Bible Commentary. Scottdale, PA: Herald Press, 2006.

Marshall, I. Howard, A. R. Millard, J. I. Packer, and D. J. Wiseman, eds. *New Bible Dictionary.* 3rd edition. Leicester, England ; Downers Grove, Ill: InterVarsity Press, 1996.

Also from Energion Publications

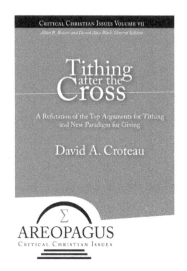

Here is essential reading for the Christian who wants to be biblically obedient!

Craig L. Blomberg, Ph.D.
Denver Seminary, Denver, CO

This book may be the catalyst for revival that the Church so desperately needs.

Lawrence E. Bray Th.D.
President,
The North American Reformed Seminary

More from Energion Publications

Personal Study
Holy Smoke! Unholy Fire	Bob McKibben	$14.99
The Jesus Paradigm	David Alan Black	$17.99
When People Speak for God	Henry Neufeld	$17.99
The Sacred Journey	Chris Surber	$11.99

Christian Living
It's All Greek to Me	David Alan Black	$3.99
Grief: Finding the Candle of Light	Jody Neufeld	$8.99
My Life Story	Becky Lynn Black	$14.99
Crossing the Street	Robert LaRochelle	$16.99
Life as Pilgrimage	David Moffett-Moore	14.99

Bible Study
Learning and Living Scripture	Lentz/Neufeld	$12.99
From Inspiration to Understanding	Edward W. H. Vick	$24.99
Philippians: A Participatory Study Guide	Bruce Epperly	$9.99
Ephesians: A Participatory Study Guide	Robert D. Cornwall	$9.99
Ecclesiastes: A Participatory Study Guide	Russell Meek	$9.99

Theology
Creation in Scripture	Herold Weiss	$12.99
Creation: the Christian Doctrine	Edward W. H. Vick	$12.99
The Politics of Witness	Allan R. Bevere	$9.99
Ultimate Allegiance	Robert D. Cornwall	$9.99
History and Christian Faith	Edward W. H. Vick	$9.99
The Journey to the Undiscovered Country	William Powell Tuck	$9.99
Process Theology	Bruce G. Epperly	$4.99

Ministry
Clergy Table Talk	Kent Ira Groff	$9.99
Out of This World	Darren McClellan	$24.99

Generous Quantity Discounts Available
Dealer Inquiries Welcome
Energion Publications — P.O. Box 841
Gonzalez, FL_ 32560
Website: http://energionpubs.com
Phone: (850) 525-3916

CPSIA information can be obtained
at www.ICGtesting.com
Printed in the USA
LVHW031505200223
739934LV00004B/383